LECTURES

ON

SCHOLASTIC PHILOSOPHY.

ROEHAMPTON
PRINTED BY JAMES STANLEY.

LECTURES

ON

SCHOLASTIC PHILOSOPHY.

BY

F. JOHN CORNOLDI, S.J.

PART I.—LOGIC.

LONDON:

BURNS AND OATES, PORTMAN STREET,

AND PATERNOSTER ROW.

1876.

NOTE.

THIS volume is translated from the second edition[*]
of the *Lezioni di Filosofia Scolastica* of F. Cornoldi,
of the Society of Jesus. It comprises the whole of
the Lectures on Logic ; the rest of the work will
be issued speedily, and the whole will form two
volumes of 300 or 350 pages each.   The author
devotes a large part of his work to Rational Physics,
discussed on scholastic principles, and it is hoped
that the work will be found useful not merely in
Colleges, but also by that large and increasing
number of readers who will be glad to be taught,
in the English language, how the Christian faith
can be shown to be in perfect harmony with all
that is really proved by modern physics.

[*] Ferrara, 1875.

CONTENTS.

INTRODUCTION.

LOGIC.

The First Part.

ON THE EFFICIENT CAUSE OF THE RATIONAL ORDER.

The Second Part.

ON THE MATERIAL CAUSE OF THE RATIONAL ORDER.

The Third Part.

The Fourth Part.

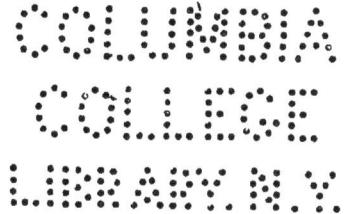
INTRODUCTORY.

LECTURE I.—PHILOSOPHY, USEFUL AND NECESSARY.

PHILOSOPHY is not merely an adornment to the human mind, but it is also of the highest advantage to man, whether he be considered as an individual or as a member of society. This assertion is supported by the authority of some of the wisest men who have lived upon the earth, and it is the teaching of reason itself.

The great writers of antiquity agree upon this subject. Thus in the Platonic dialogue on Being, we find Theodorus and Socrates conversing as follows: *Theod.* "No man, to my thinking, can claim to be called God, although some seem to have a right to be called divine; for I cannot refuse this epithet to our philosophers." *Socr.* "Friend, you are right. But it is not easy to find true philosophers." And in the fifth book of the Republic, the following is the definition given by Plato of a philosopher: "By a philosopher we understand one who studies wisdom; not this point of wisdom or that alone, but all wisdom. However, a wide distinction must be made between those who are led by curiosity to seek to become acquainted with things by their own eyes or by the

B

testimony of others, and who exercise arts, and those of whom we were speaking just now, and to whom alone I give the name of philosophers." Another passage may be quoted to show the opinion entertained by Plato of the necessity of philosophers in the State : "If the reins of civil Government are not held by philosophers, or if those who have the name of kings and potentates do not devote themselves in due degree to philosophy—if power and wisdom are not found united in the same person—there will be no hope of seeing an end put to the evils of the State and, as I further believe, of the human race."

A passage of the Tusculan Disputations may be quoted to show the mind of Cicero. This statesman, withdrawing from the cares of business and the tumult of the city, raised his mind to contemplate truth, and broke forth into the praises of philosophy. "Philosophy, guide of our life, whose voice leads us to virtue and chases vice away. Without philosophy the life of man would be nought. By philosophy States were formed, laws established, order maintained. . . . One day spent in conformity with the dictates of philosophy is better than a guilty immortality" (Tusc. Disp. v. 2).

To show the mind of Christendom upon the subject, it will be sufficient to quote the words of St. Thomas of Aquino, who divides, with Dante and Galileo, the glory of standing at the head of the genius of Italy. In the commentary of St. Thomas upon the treatise of Boethius' *De Consolatione Philosophiæ*, we read : "Philosophy renders man like to God ;" and the passage of Seneca is cited with approval in which he likens the philosopher to a God sojourning in the body of a man. Again, St. Thomas says in another place: "Plato teaches that the State is happy when ruled by a philosopher; but woe to the people whose governor is a child. And this is true; for philosophy or wisdom is the guide of life, the rule of action, showing what we should do and what we should leave undone. Seneca, in his six-teenth Epistle, says: If you would have all things subject to thee, make thyself subject to reason. And Aristotle, in the opening of his Metaphysics: To rule and to guide belongs to the Wise Man. All these maxims make it clear that it is well when the Wise rule the State, as is taught by Cicero also in the opening of his Rhetoric." The meaning is not that wisdom alone gives the right to govern, but that those who direct the State ought to be furnished with true wisdom.

The praises of philosophy may seem extravagant; but this will arise from forgetting what was under-stood by philosophy by the writers whom we have cited. The truth of what has been advanced will be admitted when it is understood that "Wisdom is the science of all things, divine and human," as Cicero expresses it (De Off. i. 43). If we apply ourselves to the consideration of man, we shall see that he is formed by nature for the knowledge of Truth and the possession of Good, and that he finds peace and perfection in these; and Philosophy furnishes wings to man, that he may fly along his appointed course. Speculative Philosophy gives him the knowledge of God and of all created things; Practical Philosophy offers the rule by which he ought to guide his actions with regard to God and man, and points out the final state of endless happiness to which his immortal soul ought to tend : a state which a kind Providence has ennobled and elevated to a supernatural character, granting gifts of grace to rational creatures in addition to all that they had by nature.

Philosophy being the Science of all things, human and divine, there is, properly speaking, no natural science which is not included in Philosophy ; so that Physics, Chemistry, Astronomy, Medicine, and Jurisprudence either are subordinate to Philosophy, or have no true claim to the name of Science.

The question may naturally occur to the reader how it happens that, for a century and more, Philosophy has been generally considered a deadly enemy to religion and civil order ? that Philosopher is almost synonymous with Dreamer and Unbeliever ? How is it that Philosophy is almost everywhere banished from the schools, so that young men acquire a mere smattering of philosophical ideas, and devote all their energies to various branches of study conducted by historical and experimental methods.

My own persuasion is that the reason will be found in the exchange by which a spiritless, lifeless substitute has been put in the place of the true Philosophy : in the overthrow of these principles of eternal truth, which were the foundation of all human Science : in the total rejection of the wisdom of past ages, and the adoption among men of the system of universal doubt, from which all Science was to spring forth, just as the universe sprang forth from God.

Luther was the originator of this system, and his followers in Philosophy have been Descartes, Spinosa, Locke, Malebranche, Kant, Fichte, Hegel, Schelling, and others; men who seem sent into the world to plunge all speculation into thick darkness, and in practical life prepare the way for the entire overthrow of Society. The essential oneness ot Philosophy—a oneness like that of truth itself—is forgotten; no blame attaches to the adoption of a set of opinions in open contradiction among themselves, and every aspirant is allowed to put together a Philosophy of his own and to call it by his name. Vanity is flattered, but a door is opened to the most palpable errors. The fatal error that the source of all certainty is to be found in doubt, may seem a trifling mistake if it be compared with more recent delusions; when applause is bestowed upon theories such as these: Being and Not Being are the same thing; I am the only existing thing, my thought is the only existing thing; outside of my thought nothing exists; God is all things; I am God.

The anarchy prevailing in Philosophy has a pernicious effect on all the sciences. Physics is not content with renouncing all concern with the essences of the substances treated by it, but is ready to give equal welcome to the most contradictory opinions concerning these essences; all which opinions may be false, while not more than one can possibly be true. Medicine undertakes to cure the diseases of man without first making itself acquainted with his physical constitution; and it is equally ready to regard him as an aggregate of inextended points, or

as a heap of inert atoms. Jurisprudence will have
nothing to do with the foundations of all justice
as laid by reason; and the like may be said of all
the sciences. It would be unfair to make this state
of things a ground of reproach against the professors
of the several sciences: for these sciences are sub-
ordinates, and ought to receive their principles from
the leading science, which is Philosophy properly so
called, and especially Metaphysics; if this be wanting,
the rest are unable to find a sure foundation.

A little consideration will show that human
knowledge in all its branches necessarily is con-
versant with the essences, powers, actions, and affections of things; and that a change in the essence
is inevitably a change of the powers and operations. This being so, what are we to think of
the attitude of indifference with which well-nigh all
schools of Philosophy of the present day regard
the rival and contradictory doctrines which prevail
concerning the essences of things? We must acknowledge that in this sea of doubt, many a ship is
wrecked on the rock of error, and that human
knowledge far from making progress is drifting back
to ignorance.

It follows from what we have said, that all who
aspire to gain high intellectual culture, and to profit
by it, do well to apply themselves to the study of
Philosophy. If this be neglected, the memory may
be stored with a mass of truths, but the mind will
not be adorned with science truly so called. Nor is
it enough to have given cursory study even to a
sound course of Philosophy: to gain the full benefit

of their labour, even proficients find it necessary to return again and again to the beginning; even those who hold a front place in the ranks of learning do well to renew their familiarity with these principles upon which all knowledge rests.

There is a special reason at the present time why Philosophy should be studied by young men, for it will serve as a sword and shield to defend them against the assaults of the designing to which they are exposed. Youth is naturally frank, and does not readily suspect fraud in others, and on this account it is the more liable to be led astray; but it is hard to deceive one who is well grounded in Philosophy, and, on this account, the materialistic and atheistic writers of the day use every endeavour to hinder men from reading the works of sound philosophers.

The present volume is no more than a compendium of the subject. An endeavour has been made to avoid the reproach, *Compendia sunt dispendia*, by the omission of all useless questions and all which seemed too clear to need explanation. Care has also been taken in the arrangement to avoid loss of time by useless repetitions.

LECTURE II.—DEFINITION OF PHILOSOPHY. DIVISIONS.

Philosophy defined.—Philosophy is the pursuit and love of wisdom, and, as explained in the preceding Lecture, it embraces all those branches of knowledge

to which the name of Science can be applied. The
name of Science is inapplicable to knowledge which
is purely experimental, or which is obtained through
the testimony of others, and by way of authority.
Science is evident and certain knowledge, founded
on acquaintance with the causes of the objects
known. It belongs to another place to develope
fully the different parts of this definition; it will be
sufficient here to say that Science concerns itself
directly with Universals and indirectly with Singulars.
Thus, I frame the following argument: *Every intellectual soul is immortal; but every human soul is
intellectual; therefore, every human soul is immortal.*
My knowledge of this last universal proposition is
scientific, and Science is concerned *directly* with
propositions such as this; but, while the reason is
pronouncing this judgment, it is *indirectly* pronouncing that Peter, who has an intellectual soul,
has an immortal soul. Thus the soul of man, looked
at universally, is considered by science *directly*, but
the particular soul of Peter is considered *indirectly*.
The same remarks apply to all scientific knowledge
of things. What we have here said applies to the
case of the human intellect and its knowledge of
finite beings; for if we are considering the Infinite
and Perfect Being, this general doctrine must be
applied in a particular man, as will be seen in the
proper place.

Division.—The act of the intellect may be considered in a twofold manner: first, in so far as it
knows being; secondly, in so far as it is the idea
or pattern of that which can be done by the will,

whether immediately or by means of the powers subordinated to it. The first aspect gives us speculative knowledge; for example, *The world is finite :* the second aspect gives practical knowledge; for example, *A creature ought to honour the Creator.* The most general division of Philosophy and Science is then into Speculative Philosophy or Science, and Practical Philosophy or Science. This division is perfect, for all scientific knowledge falls under one or other of the members. And in fact nothing can exist, nor can be known by man, but what either cannot be done by man or can be done by him ; the first branch belongs to Speculative Science; the second to Practical Science.

Divisions of Speculative Philosophy or Science.— These may conveniently be divided according to the various manners of framing Universals, by *abstracting* or prescinding from matter. That this may be understood, as far as is here necessary, let us take a particular man who exists in some determinate place and time and who has *this* flesh and *these* bones, and whose name is Cæsar. I can touch him, hear him, see him ; that is to say, he is a Singular, concerning whom I can have that experimental knowledge which is not Science. Let us make a first mental abstraction, and abstain from considering whatever is individual in Cæsar, whatever is restricted to place and determined by time ; let the intellect rest on the essence of man, which is common to all men, whether existing or possible, and which is accordingly universal. In this abstract way of considering Cæsar, I truly prescind from the individual matter of Cæsar, but I cannot prescind from matter conceived universally, because a body belongs to the *Essence* of man. What is here said of the knowledge of Cæsar may be said of the knowledge of any brute, plant, or mineral. The first abstraction will take away from our thoughts the individual matter, but not matter in general. The whole body of knowledge of this kind taken together gives the first part of Speculative Philosophy, or the Science of Physics. The vastness of the field will be seen at once; wherefore, there will be a gain in clearness if we make a further division, and distinguish (1) material substance *in genere*, abstracting from individual matter; this will give the science of General Physics. (2) Corporal substance devoid of life is the object of Mineralogy. (3) Corporal substance living with no more than vegetative life is discussed by Botany. (4) Corporal substance further endowed with sensitive life belongs to Zoology. (5) Anthropology treats of corporal substance in which is a principle of rational life. The four parts make up what we may call Rational Physics, to distinguish the Science from Physics treated by experimental or historical methods, which is no true Science. '

Although no further abstraction is possible beyond matter, yet in universal matter we may confine our attention to its *quantity* alone. This *quantity*, which may be *continuous* or *discrete*, affords the object of the second part of Speculative Philosophy, which is Mathematics.

Lastly, the intellect of man raises itself altogether

above matter and its material properties, and contemplates Being independently of all matter. Being, when contemplated in this manner, is the object of Metaphysics, which is so called because it transcends all that is physical or corporeal. Now the Being which can thus be contemplated in itself apart from all matter may be (1) such as is capable of accompanying matter, although it can exist in independence of matter; this is the object of the first part of Metaphysics, which is called the First Philosophy, Philosophia Prima, because it is conveniently treated even before Physics. Or this Being may be (2) wholly immaterial and utterly independent of matter; and thus we have the Science of Pure Spirits and of God, which constitutes the second part of Metaphysics: this, on account of its sublimity, is usually treated in the last place. And thus the division of Speculative Philosophy is complete.

Divisions of Practical Philosophy or Science.— These have for their object the order which man can produce among (1) his own actions, so far as they conform with law and are directed to the end of man; or (2) among his actions, so far as they promote the physical well-being of his person; or (3) so far as they affect bodily substance external to the man. Putting aside the consideration of these two last parts of practical Science, as not suitable for treatment here, we confine ourselves to the Practical Science of the Moral Order. This admits of division into various parts, as follows. We may speak (*a*) of the moral order in general, considering its various causes, efficient, material, formal, and final: thus, we have Ethics. Coming down to the *special* conditions of man considered as a moral being we may (*b*) treat him as an individual, when the Science will be that which anciently was called *Monastica*; or as member of a family, the object of Economics; or finally as member of society, the object of Politics.

Logic.—In order to treat the Sciences which we have named, it is necessary in the first place to treat of Logic, the Instrument of Knowledge, as it is called. This Science teaches man how to order aright the acts of his intellect in the pursuit of truth and acquirement of real Science, on which account it is termed Rational Science (λόγος, word, or reason). It is true that all men, being endowed with reason, are masters of a natural Logic, by which they are naturally guided to truth; but this natural Logic is very imperfect in most men, because they neglect the cultivation of the mind, and because, under the influence of passion, they lose sight of the principles which govern human reasoning, and are hindered from applying them in due manner. The result is that among those man who have not studied the artificial Logic which is given in the schools, very few are free from gross errors on the most important subjects. And why should not that which is said regarding Rhetoric and the liberal arts be also said concerning the mode of reasoning, so as to secure the attainment of truth and the requirement of Science? Artificial Logic, it is true, does no more than give an exact and methodical shape to those rules which have already been delivered by Natural Logic; but in like manner, Rhetoric derives from nature its precepts for the right use of language; and

Sculpture and Painting give a methodical shape to those rules which nature has already delivered for representing objects on canvas or in marble. And what speaker is perfect without the study of Rhetoric? What Painter or Sculptor who has not mastered the rules of his art? And the same, or even more, must be said of Logic; for the task of putting due order into the discourse of the mind is far more difficult than is success in speaking, or in the Painter's or Sculptor's arts.

Another reason proving the peculiar advantage of the study of Logic at the present time is found in the wide diffusion of error and the scarcity of sound instruction. In times of pestilence, men are forced to live in the company of the plague-stricken, and to breathe the deadly air of infection, and prudence suggests the use of remedies which may promise to be effectual in warding off the danger. At the present time a similar precaution must be taken in the realm of Science, under penalty of a fall into pernicious error. Among the remedies suitable in this case the study of Logic holds the first place, for it gives a delicacy of intellectual touch to distinguish truth and falsehood, and a peculiar power of discerning truth from error, and of unmasking falsehood when it lurks under the mask of truth.

LOGIC.

THE FIRST PART.

On the Efficient Cause of the Rational Order.

LECTURE III.—THE EFFICIENT CAUSE OF THE '
RATIONAL ORDER.

THE Efficient Cause of the Rational Order is Man,
and we must here give a short general notion of what
man is, for this is a necessary introduction to what we
have to say in Logic. Man is defined a rational
animal : he is a complete substance, composed of two
incomplete substances, the one of which is matter,
while the other is the soul. Man is a miniature of
the world, for he partakes in the nature of all other
beings. The principle of all activity in a man is the
human soul which informs his body ; it is the principle
alike of his vegetable life, his sensitive life, and his
intellectual life.

Man being a substance which enjoys vegetable
life, we find in him the faculties which we find less
perfectly in plants. Thus we have in him *nutrition,*
growth, and generation.

Man being a substance which enjoys sensitive life,
we find in him the faculties which we find in brutes.

Thus man possesses the same cognitive power as brutes, and accordingly he has the five senses, sight, hearing, smell, taste, and touch, with which he renders external bodily objects present to himself; or, to use a better phrase, by means of which all bodily substances *join themselves* to man in various ways, and thus bring home to him his own knowledge. In addition to the five external senses, man is furnished with an interior sense, *sensus intimus*, by which he feels the modifications of his external senses and those which are undergone internally by his own organism; and thus he obtains matter for the formation of those phantasms by which the cognition of animals is completed.

In man, considered as a mere animal, there is a sensible appetitive faculty corresponding to this sensible cognoscitive faculty; and by this he tends towards whatever is presented to the sense as suitable or *good;* this appetitive faculty includes the power of locomotion, by which the man moves his own limbs.

Lastly, man, considered as rational, possesses some faculties peculiar to himself and superior to those which have been mentioned. Two of these peculiar faculties must be here distinguished : first the *Intellect,* and secondly the *Will,* faculties which are immaterial and spiritual. The following account of these faculties must be sufficient for the present. Things unite themselves to man's intellect, and man's knowledge of them arises from this union, and it consists in a spiritual image formed from the Intellect and called a *Word.* It is with and by a word that the Intellect knows all that it does know. But the things by which man is surrounded being material or corporeal, and the Intellect being an immaterial or incorporeal faculty, it is impossible that an immediate union should take place between the former and the latter; but the union is accomplished by means of *species intelligibiles*, formed in the Intellect itself and being representatives of exterior things.

The Intellect, when informed by the *species intelligibilis* of a thing, simply names that thing to itself with a mental word. For example: the eye sees a lion, and thus there arises an external sensation; a phantasm of the lion is formed in the imagination, and in the Intellect the *species intelligibilis*, or spiritual representation of the lion comes into being; whereupon the Intellect, first by a simple word, says in and to itself, *Lion.** Then, having the *species intelligibiles* of *lion*, *fierce* and *tame*, the Intellect produces a complex word, saying, *the lion is fierce*, or, *the lion is not tame*. The first of these complex words expresses a positive judgment by which the Intellect affirms identity; the second a negative judgment in which identity is denied. I have purposely used the words *affirm* and *deny*, for merely to see in the mind the agreement of *fierce* with *lion*, or the disagreement of *tame* from *lion*, is

---

* A large number of modern philosophers following the error of Descartes, confound the *Idea* with the *Species Intelligibilis*, or Word of the Mind; which confusion naturally leads to other mistakes. The *Idea* of a thing or of an action, as we shall see hereafter, is the immaterial pattern in which it is formed, and it belongs not to speculative but to practical science. This was the sense in which the word was used by all great philosophers and theologians up to the time of Descartes.

not a judgment as some have erroneously taught. Thirdly, the Intellect passes from one Complex Word or from one Judgment, to another, compares them, and either unites or separates them, and forms a new Complex Word or Judgment, resulting from the comparison. This internal Discourse of the Intellect is called Reasoning. The Intellect discourses as follows : *No Lion is biped, but every bird is biped; therefore no Lion is a Bird.* This discourse is called Reasoning, and it has for its fruit or end to know the truth of things in a clear and distinct manner. The order in which these acts of the Intellect should be arranged to attain this end, is called the Logical or Rational Order, and it is with this that we shall be occupied in Logic.

In the commencement of a course of Philosophy it is difficult to treat of the Logical Order considered in itself ; but it is easy to treat of it in its outward manifestations and signs, which are words. The Simple Word of the Intellect has for its sign those simple words of the mouth which are called terms : the sign of the complex Word of the Intellect, or of a Judgment, is a Proposition in which the substantive verb *is* denotes the mental affirmation of identity, and *is not* its mental negation. Lastly, the sign of internal discourse or reasoning is the Syllogism. We shall therefore follow the Logical Order in treating of Terms, Propositions, and Syllogisms.

The Intellect in man is then an immaterial cognoscitive faculty, by means of which man unites to himself all things and knows them : to this there corresponds the appetitive faculty which is called the

C

Will, by which man tends towards that which he knows and embraces it, so far as he knows it to be suitable or *good* for himself. This appetitive faculty, receives its illumination from the Intellect, and in this it differs from the lower appetitive faculty which of itself tends *necessarily* towards that which sense declares to be good : but it is endowed with liberty, or is able to incline towards either of two goods, whether they be equal, or one greater than the other ; and consequently is able to choose or not to choose anything whatever which comes before it in the character of a finite good. And as the name of Understanding is given to the act by which the Intellect, in forming a Word, makes the known thing to be its own, and by its Word gives the thing a spiritual existence ; so the name of love is given to the act by which the Will tends towards an object and unites it with itself.

We have hitherto made no mention of Memory or of Reason, for our aim has been to give a brief sketch of those faculties which are really distinct. Now Memory is not a distinct faculty in man, whether considered as animal or as rational. But in man, so far as he is animal, it is nothing but the Imagination, so far as this retains the *Species* or sensible images of things which have been known by the formation of a mental Word. Reason is the same Intellect which is called Intelligence when it sees the truth by a single act, and has the name of Reason when it is forced to use reasoning to attain the truth.

THE SECOND PART.

On the Material Cause of the Rational Order.

LECTURE IV.—DEFINITIONS AND DIVISIONS OF TERMS.

Matter of Rational Order.—Whatever is capable of putting on the character of a subject to receive any actualization, modification, and order, of whatever kind, is commonly called by the generic name of *Matter;* and the actualization, modification, and order, be they what they may, receive the name of *Form.* These terms are not employed with reference to corporeal things alone, but the distinction of Matter and Form has place also in our thoughts. This being so, we say that those acts of the Intellect which admit of being arranged suitably for the attainment of truth are reckoned as Matter, or as the Material Cause of the Rational Order. And just as we remarked in the preceding Lecture that the acts of the Intellect can be discussed more conveniently by the use of their signs, so here we shall take *Term* and *Proposition* as being the Matter of the Rational Order.*

Definition and Division of Term.—(a). The word *Term* may be defined either absolutely or with refer-

---

* The endeavour made by some modern philosophers to treat internal acts *ex professo* in Logic, has caused great confusion to the student. Beginners in philosophy are like babes, standing in need of simple food.

ence to the Rational Order. Taken absolutely, it is
the external sign of a thing which has become the
object of thought by a simple internal word ; thus
lion, virtue, good, strong, are Terms. Considered relatively, it is defined by Aristotle, that into which
every proposition is resolved, as into Subject and
Predicate. Let us, for example, take the proposition,
The wise man is worthy of honour. *The wise man*
is subject (subjicitur) to that which follows, namely,
worthy of honour. To be *worthy of honour* is attributed to the subject (attribuitur subjecto, de eo
prædicatur), and is therefore called the attribute or
predicate. If this proposition be analyzed it will
divide into Subject and Predicate, which are united
by the verb *is,* so as to form one whole. Hence, *wise
man* will be one term, *worthy of honour* will be the
other, and the substantive verb *is* is neither a term
nor part of a term, but is the link joining one term
to the other.

(*b*). Very many divisions may be given of terms.
The following will suffice.

I. *Terms* may be *univocal, equivocal,* or *analogous :*
which must not be understood as though an univocal
term could not be also equivocal or analogous ; but
the meaning is that a term may be taken univocally,
equivocally, or analogically.

A term is taken univocally when it is used in two
or more instances to the same sense. Thus *man* is
used univocally of Peter, Paul, and Andrew, for it is
used in the same sense in all three instances.

A term is taken equivocally when it is used in
two or more instances in totally different significa-

tions. Thus the terms *bear*, *bull*, *fish* are used equivocally of the animals and the constellations.

When a term is applied to two or more things in senses which in some respects are identical and in some respects different, the term is taken analogically. There are two sorts of analogy of terms—analogy of attribution and analogy of proportion. Analogy of attribution is found between terms which signify things of different natures, but all having some connection with some one thing. Thus the word *healthful* may be applied to a medicine, to a locality, food, complexion, exercise, a dwelling, and to an animal: the earlier applications being connected with the last either by way of cause or by way of sign. Analogy of proportion exists when a term is used in two essentially distinct senses, which senses nevertheless stand in similar relations to two other terms. Thus we speak of the *smile* of a man and of a *smiling* meadow, because the expression of the features bears to the man a relation similar to that borne to the meadow by the bright array of flowers and waving grass. It is on a like principle that a cruel man is called a Nero, a bold man is called a lion, and so on.

2. Secondly, terms are divided into *singular, universal, transcendental*, and *particular*.

A *singular* term is that which admits of being applied to a single individual only: *e.g.*, Julius Cæsar, this man, that chair, and the like.

A *universal* term is that which admits of being applied *univocally* to many. *Univocal* application may be *specific, generic, differential, proper*, or *accidental*, which words will now be explained.

A *specific* term is that which indicates the whole essence of the objects to which it is applied. Thus the term *man* indicates that Peter, Antonio, Cæsar, to whom I apply it, is a rational animal. This is the signification of the term man, and is one which comprises the whole essence of the objects to which it is applied.

A *generic* term is that which indicates that part only of the essence which is conceived as undetermined and determinable. Thus the term *animal* is generic, because it indicates that part of the essence of man which is determined by the other part, *rational.*

A *differential* term is that which indicates that part of the essence which is conceived as determining the genus. Thus *rational* is a differential term.

A *proper* term is that which indicates something which is inseparable from the whole essence, and can only be applied to things which have the same essence. Thus the power of reasoning is *proper* to man, and belongs to all men, and to men only.

An *accidental* term is that which indicates something which does not belong to the essence and may be separated from it. Thus *white* applied to a man would be an accidental term, for it would be applicable to some and not to others.

The five things which are indicated by these five terms, *genus, species, difference, property,* and *accident,* are called *universals,* and also *predicables.* They are called *universals* because many things participate or can participate in them. Thus many things have the same *genus, species, difference, property,* and *accident.*

They are also called *predicables* because in every proposition that predicate which is capable of being applied univocally to many things, must be either *genus, species, difference, property,* or *accident.*

A *transcendental* term can be applied not only to many things but to everything that exists or can exist, though this application is not always universal. A transcendental is that which is expressed by a transcendental term. Strictly speaking, there are only four transcendental terms: Being, the one, the true, and the good; the first of these terms indicates the transcendental itself, and the other three denote attributes of it. Everything that exists has being, and in as far as it has being is one, true, and good; though in other-respects and in other senses it may be said to be manifold, false, and bad.

A *particular* term is nothing but a *universal* or *transcendental* term, taken with a limitation, which is indicated by some particle. Thus *some beings, several men,* are particular terms; but if the particle were to restrict the universal or transcendental term to a single individual, as, *that man, this dog,* it would become a *singular* term according to our former explanation.

3. Thirdly, terms are divided into *absolute* terms, such as *man,* which are applied to the thing considered in itself; and, *relative* terms, such as master, servants, father, son, which are applied to the thing considered in relation to some other.

4. Finally, passing over less important distinctions, terms are divided into *abstract* and *concrete*: an *abstract* term is one which expresses a quality apart

from the being of its object, as *humanity, wisdom, whiteness.* A *concrete* term expresses quality in union with being, as *man, learned, white.*

This will suffice for the divisions of terms.

LECTURE V.—ON DEFINITION AND DIVISION.

Definition and the rules which ensure its correctness.
—Speaking generally, a definition is a composite term which encloses the thing defined, as it were, within certain *limits* and distinguishes it from all other things. Definitions are *nominal* or *real.* The first are of words, and describe their etymology or the sense in which they are used, whether ordinary or proper to the person writing or speaking. The second are of things, and describe their origin, or their properties, or their complete essence, pointing out their *genus proximum* and *ultima differentia.* These last only are the definitions of philosophy, and are those with which we are specially concerned.

(*a*) A philosophical definition then is that term in a proposition which is called the predicate and not the whole of the proposition, and cannot be simple, but is composed of several terms, each of which might itself be a predicate. For example in the proposition, *man is a rational animal,* the predicate *rational animal* is the definition, and the subject *man* is the thing defined.

(*b*) In the second place a definition should be as clear as possible, because its object is to give a clear

conception of the thing defined. But this clearness
is relative, and it is absurd to expect that philosophical definitions should be self-evident to unedu-
cated minds. It is a mistake, therefore, to reject
many true philosophical definitions, as some have
done, because they are difficult of comprehension, and
fix instead upon definitions which though possessing a
fallacious clearness are neither philosophical nor true.
The following are instances of such clear and false
definitions : *Living corporeal substance is an aggregate
of atoms symmetrically arranged. The soul is the
activity of the atoms which compose the brain.*

(*c*) In the third place a definition should be
distinct. It should ascribe to the thing defined that
which is peculiar to it only, and thus produce a
distinct conception, such as shall distinguish it from
any other thing. Thus to say, *Virtue is a quality of
the soul,* would be a bad definition, for the same
could apply to vice. The ultimate difference of the
thing defined must therefore be expressed in the
definition in such a manner that it shall be impossible
to apply it to anything else. I say this because the
common teaching that a perfect definition ought to
point out the *genus proximum* and *ultima differentia*
of the thing defined, though perfectly correct, is in
many cases extremely difficult to put in practice.
Here it is to be observed that there are many genera
(the *determinable* part of the essence of things) and
many differences (the *determining* part). And under
the head *transcendental,* which is *being,* and which
extends to everything, may be named two genera of
the greatest extent, that of *substance,* or being which

exists in itself, and *accident*, or being which necessarily inheres in some other as its subject; and these genera comprise innumerable sub-genera, which it would be tedious and useless to mention here. But that every one may see the force of the words *primary* and *ultimate* applied to *genus* and *difference* we give here the category of substance:

	Substance.	
Composite.		Simple.
	Body.	
Animate.		Inanimate.
	Living Being.	
Sensitive.		Insensitive.
	Animal.	
Rational.		Irrational.
	Man.	

The word substance indicates the *genus supremum*, because it stands immediately under the transcendental, being, and not under any other *genus*. The words in the centre column : *body, living being, animal*, are at once the subordinate genus and the things defined ; the two lateral columns give the differentiæ, which together with the genera give the species and the perfect definitions. If I wish to define body I say, *Body is composite substance.* If I wish to define a *living being* I say, *A living being is an animate body.* To define *animal* I should say, *An animal is a sensitive living being.* If I define *man* I say, *Man is a rational animal.* But since man cannot be a genus, because the conception of man excludes the addition of any determining essence (differentia), it follows that under man there can only be individuals, and *man* is the ultimate species. And that there may be no confusion with regard to our first principles, let us note that when we say that a corporeal living being is animate corporeal substance, we mean corporeal substance endued with the vital principle which (even though insensitive) is in general terms called soul.

(*d*) Hence it follows that we cannot give a true definition : (1) of those things which have not genus and differentia, therefore *transcendental, substance,* and *accident,* cannot be philosophically defined, though they can be described and to a certain extent explained, while on the other hand specific substances and determined accidents can perfectly be defined ; (2) that definitions should not be given of things which are obvious, for this creates confusion rather than clearness ; (3) that true definitions cannot be given of things which are not so known that their essence can be indicated, and therefore those scientific men (and they are many) who abstract the phenomena from the essence of things, and stop short at the former, cannot give true philosophical definitions.

Now any one who attentively considers what we have said on this subject of definition will see how useful it is, and how right the ancients were in ranking *definitions* among the principal *modes* or *instruments* of knowledge. Any one who discourses of the sciences without being careful to define exactly, runs the risk of falling into serious errors at every step.

Division, and the rules that must be observed to make it correctly.—Division, as appears from the name itself, is the distribution of a whole into those parts of which it is, or can be conceived to be, composed. The different denominations of *wholes* are of little importance; it is enough for us to know that any sort of thing whether ideal, or real, or existing, or possible, in which various parts can be considered, is capable of division. But this does not imply that this division can always be made in fact, as well as by the mind, for many things can be mentally divided which are indivisible in fact. And now to come to the rules which govern division.

(*a*) *Division* should be expressed in a proposition in which the term which forms the subject is the thing divided, and the term which forms the predicate the divisor.

(*b*) It should be *adequate*, that is it should contain neither more nor less than the thing divided. Thus it would not be an adequate division of corporeal substance to say it is divided into sensitive and rational organisms; for one part, inorganic corporeal substance, would be wanting.

(*c*) The parts of the *thing divided* must mutually exclude each other, and cannot include any other. Thus it would be incorrect to divide the earth into Europe, Asia, Africa, America, Australia, and Italy; because Italy is included in Europe.

(*d*) No part of the *divisor* can by itself equal the *thing divided.* Thus to say that animal life is divided into sensitive being and rational being would be clearly a bad division, for sensitive being is co-extensive with animal life, and what is rational is also sensitive.

(*e*) Finally division should also be as simple, and consist of as few members, as possible. Afterwards each member of the division may itself become the subject of a fresh division, and this may he repeated as often as it is necessary or convenient. This is the method pursued in works on scientific subjects such as physics, medicine, &c. They begin with the more general considerations and descend to particulars, following the order of the subordination of things.

LECTURE VI.—OF THE DEFINITION AND DIVISION OF PROPOSITIONS.

Propositions.—As terms are the signs of the simple *verbum mentale*, so are propositions the signs of the complex *verbum mentale* or *judgment* by which the intellect *pronounces* upon a thing, and either affirms or denies it, as we said in the third Lecture. For this reason Aristotle called a proposition an *interpretation*, because it interprets the judgment of the intellect. It is defined thus : *A proposition is a sentence in which one term is joined to another or disjoined from it.* I say *term*, and not *thing*, because often both terms express the same thing, and because it is not things, but the signs of things, which a proposition unites or separates. The conjunction which unites the two terms is the substantive verb *is :* when they are disjoined the negative *is not* is used. This conjunction is explicit, as thus : *A wise man is more estimable than a rich man;* or implicit as : *A wise man despises flattery.* And all verbs have the property of implicitly containing this substantive verb : thus, *he loves,* is logically equivalent to *he is loving : he tolerates* to *he is tolerating,* and so on.

Therefore not only may the conjunction be often implicit, but frequently the subject, predicate, and copula, are implied in a single word, and thus the words *veni; vidi; vici;* are three propositions.

The division of propositions.—There are many divisions corresponding to the view taken of the proposition. Hence :

1. Considered as regards their nature on the two terms of which they consist, propositions are divided into : (*a*) necessary or analytic; (*b*) contingent or synthetic. In the first the predicate is included in the essence of the subject; for example : *Man is endowed with reason; Virtue adorns a man :* these propositions are seen to be true by simply analyzing the terms. In the second the predicate is not included in the essence of the subject; for example : *Columbus discovered America; Cæsar conquered Gaul; Cicero existed.* It must be observed that here by *existence* is meant that which constitutes it in the *ideal* order, abstracting *existence* from being in itself. Hence it is plain that the conception of Cicero does not include his existence, and the proposition *Cicero existed* is synthetic and contingent. Therefore, since the predicate and the subject cannot in such propositions be united by considering the terms alone, to join them we must resort to some extrinsic motive; for example, experience or autho-

rity. By the ancients necessary and analytic propositions were called, *nota in se;* and the contingent and synthetic, *non nota in se.*

2. Considered in regard to our knowledge, propositions are called (*a*) *clear*, that which is easy to understand: (*b*) *obscure*, which is the contrary: (*c*) *evident*, when their truth is seen at once without the need of explanation: these were called by the ancients *nota quoad nos.* · Thus the proposition, *The whole is greater than any part*, is evident; but the proposition, *The square of a hypotenuse is equal to the sum of the squares of the sides*, is not evident. It is true that such propositions as this latter are often called *mediately* evident, that is, evident through demonstration; but in common language they are certainly not called *simply* evident; (*d*) *non-evident* which is the contrary of *c*.

3. Considered in regard to the quantity of the terms, propositions are divided into *universal, singular, particular, indefinite.* (*a*) They are *universal* when the subject is a universal term, for example: *Every man has within him an immortal soul:* (*b*) *singular* when the subject is a singular term : *Cicero was the greatest of orators.* (*c*) *Particular* when the subject is particular: *some children degenerate from their parents:* (*d*) *indefinite* when the subject is so taken that it is not apparent whether it is taken in a universal or a particular sense, for example: *On this earth man walks in a valley of tears. Man* is evidently a universal term when accompanied by the pronouns *all* or *no:* if the pronoun is *some*, it is particular: if *this*, it is singular: when there is

no pronoun it is indefinite. However, here it must be observed that in common language there are three kinds of indefinite propositions which are treated as universal. (1) Those which have a metaphysical universality which excludes all exceptions as : *Man is a contingent being.* (2) Those which have a physical universality from which there can be no exception without derogation of physical laws, as : *A hand that is severed from the body cannot be re-united.* (3) Those, finally, which have a moral universality, the exceptions to which, if not rare, yet depend upon human freedom, as : *Mothers love their children.*

4. Considered as regards quality, propositions are divided (*a*) into *affirmative*, (*b*) into *negative* propositions : *A sensible youth is studious; A guilty man is not happy.* Of these we have already spoken.

5. Considered with regard to the things or objects they express, propositions are divided into *true* and *false:* (*a*) *true* when they enunciate that which is ; for example, *The body is composite;* (*b*) false in the contrary case, as, *Thought is a vibration of the molecules of the brain.* And here I observe that if a proposition expresses the composite word of the mind, or the judgment, though not the truth of things, it is simply called *false;* but if it does not express the word of the mind it is called a *lie,* whether it expresses the truth of things and is true, or does not express it, and is false. Thus it is possible to lie though saying what is true. For example, a man who judges in his mind that he has not seen the king, though he really has, and

affirms, *I have seen the king*, lies, though the proposition is true.

6. Finally, considered as regards their contents,
propositions are divided into (*a*) *simple*, if they neither
contain nor therefore can be resolved into other
propositions; as, *The verbum mentale is spiritual;*
and (*b*) *composite*, when they do contain other propositions into which they can be resolved. Often a
composite proposition is as it were a whole capable
of being divided into many parts, because there are
others belonging to it. Such are: (*a*) *copulative*
propositions; which have more than one subject or
more than one predicate collected in a single term
by means of some negative or affirmative particle
(often suppressed), for example: *Both mankind and
brutes have a sensitive soul. Neither men nor brutes
consist of a mere aggregate of atoms. Italy has produced first-rate men both in war and in peace.* Concerning these kinds of propositions a warning is
necessary that they must not be called true, unless
the conjunction on the separation applies truly to all
the parts. This agrees with the general proverb:
Bonum ex integra causa, malum ex quocumque defectu.

(*b*) *Causal* propositions, in which the predicate
indicates the reason of its union with the subject;
for example: *Man's soul is incorporeal, because its
operations are immaterial:* this will be called true if
the reason assigned be true. Therefore in the contrary case it is called false, for though the predicate
applies to the subject, it is for a different motive.

(*c*) *Disjunctive* propositions, in which several predicates (sometimes subjects also) are included in a

D

single term by means of a disjunctive particle ; for example: *Madness depends either on the mind or on the body.* To make this kind of proposition true one of the two or more predicates must apply to the subject.

(*d*) *Conditional* propositions, in which something is affirmed or denied hypothetically, not absolutely ; for example. *If this man is still able to feel, he is alive.* Concerning these propositions it is useful to remark in the first place that, for them to be true, the existence of the hypotheses or conditions is not necessary, but the *nexus* between the *condition* or *antecedent*, and the *conditioned* or *consequent* is necessary. In the second place, that these propositions are really composite, and any one who does not see this need only change them into causal equivalents to make it perfectly evident.

LECTURE VII.—THE PROPERTIES OF PROPOSITIONS.

The principal properties of propositions.—There are three: (1) *equivalence;* (2) *opposition;* (3) *convertibility.*

The definition of the simple properties of propositions, and the divisions which result from them.

1. *Equivalence* is the identity which subsists between various propositions. Equivalent propositions are divided into (*a*) those which are equivalent by a simple change of words ; for example : *All obligations are in regard to possible acts ;* which is equivalent to, *There is no obligation which does not regard a possible act :* (*b*) those which are equivalent because they

belong to a whole which can resolve itself into parts, and these parts taken together are, as has been before observed, equivalent to the whole. Such are *universal affirmative* propositions; for example : *All men natu-rally desire knowledge;* which is equivalent to the sum of all the *singular* propositions, *This man naturally desires to know this thing,* &c., in which single men are indicated. Such are *universal negatives;* for example ; *No whole can exist without one of its essen-tial parts;* this is equivalent to the sum of the singular negatives : *This whole (man) cannot exist without one of his essential parts (soul)—this whole (circle) cannot exist without one of its essential parts (periphery).* Such are *particular affirmatives : Some one must be governor of the city ;* this is equivalent to, *Either this one or that one or some one else must be governor of the city.* And the same applies to *particular negatives.*

2. *Opposition* is the contrast between two propo-sitions which have the same subject and the same predicate. By means of this property they are divided into contraries, contradictories, subalterns, and sub-contraries. The following plan will serve to make this clearer.

A.   Contraries.   E.

Subalterns.   *Contradictories.*   Subalterns.
    Contradictories.

I.   Sub-Contraries.   O.

A indicates the *universal affirmative* proposition. E the *universal negative.* I the *particular affirmative.* O the *particular negative.*

(*a*) The contradictories AO and EI are those whose *opposition is both in quality and in quantity;* for example : *Every inferior can abrogate the law of the superior,* of which, *Certain inferiors cannot abrogate the law of the superior,* is the. contradictory. Or, *No inferior can abrogate the law of the superior;* of which the contradictory is, *Certain inferiors can abrogate the law of the superior.* These *contradictories* can never be both true nor both false, since from the truth of one the falsehood of the other is immediately inferred, and *vice versa.* The reason of which is that if they were both together, true or false, we should be obliged both to affirm and deny something of a thing, in the same relation, which is absurd. Thus if the two first were true, there would be some one who in virtue of O *can abrogate the law of the superior,* and this same person in virtue of the truth of A *could not abrogate this same law.*

(*b*) *Contraries,* indicated by AE, are those which are universal, and whose opposition is in their quality ; for example : *Every one who acts upon his rights injures others;* of which, *Every one who acts upon his rights does not injure others,* is the contrary. These *contrary* propositions cannot be both at once true, for the reason given in the case of *contradictory* ones ; but sometimes they may both be false, and thus the falseness of one may be inferred from the truth of the other, but from the falseness of one it is not always allowable to deduce the truth of the other.

. (*c*) *Subalterns*, indicated by AI and EO, differ in *quantity* only; for example: *Every friend is known by his actions;* to which corresponds, *Some friends are known by their actions:* or, *No one likes conversing with fools;* which corresponds with, *Some one does not like conversing with fools.*

Subalterns can, both together, be true or false, from which it follows, first, that the truth of one. cannot logically be inferred from the falsity of the other, or *vice versa;* and, secondly, that their opposition is more nominal than real.

(*d*) *Sub-contraries*, indicated by IO, are *particular*, and differ from each other in quality only; for example: *Some villains are thought well of;* to which, *Some villains are not thought well of*, corresponds. Both may sometimes be true together; but both together can never be false, because in that case their *universal contradictories* would both be true, and thus two *contraries* would be true at once, which is impossible. Therefore the truth of one may be at once inferred from the falsity of the other, but not *vice versa.*

3. *Convertibility* is *that property in propositions by which the subject can be converted into the predicate and the predicate into the subject.* Some are capable of *simple* conversion, some of *accidental*.

(*a*) It is *simple* conversion when the same quantity and quality are retained; this can be done in E and I; for example: *No body is indivisible;* from the conversion of which it is inferred, *Therefore nothing indivisible is a body.*

(*b*) It is *accidental* conversion when the quality is

retained but the quantity is changed; this can be done in A and E; for example: *Every rich man can be of use to his neighbour;* from the conversion of which it is inferred, *Therefore a man who is useful to his neighbour may be rich.*

THE THIRD PART.

LECTURE VIII.—OF THE FORMAL CAUSE OF THE RATIONAL ORDER.

The formal cause of the rational order.—"It is that disposition according to which the acts of the intellect ought to be produced in order to know a truth not already known." The acts which form the matter of this disposition, are the *simple* word of the mind which is also called the *simple apprehension of the thing*, and the composite word which is the *judgment*. These two things were treated of in speaking of their *signs*, which are terms and propositions. The mental disposition which we are now going to study is that which is called ratiocination, and its sign is the syllogism.

The definition of the syllogism.—In general terms the *syllogism* may be called *the demonstration of truth* because it points out to us, or demonstrates the truth. It is called more accurately by Aristotle,* "a sentence, in which some things being affirmed, others must necessarily follow from that affirmation." We will call it: *A disposition of terms and propositions arranged in such a manner that from what is known that which is unknown is necessarily deduced.* We have said *terms* in the first place, and *propositions* in the second, because *terms* may be regarded as the *remote*, and propositions as the *proximate*, matter of the syllogism.

* I. Analyt. c. I.

The syllogism then has (1) three terms so distributed in three propositions that each one shall be repeated twice.

Every incorruptible soul is immortal; but every human soul is an incorruptible soul; therefore every human soul is immortal.

2. Of these three terms one is called the comparative or *middle* term with which the other two which are called *extreme* terms are compared. That one of these terms which in the final inferred proposition (there called the *illation* or *conclusion*) forms the *predicate* is called the *major extreme*, and that which forms the *subject* the *minor extreme*. The reason of their being so denominated is that generally in universal affirmative propositions, which, being more perfect than negative ones, supply the appellation, the *predicate* has *greater* extension than the *subject*, and consequently the *subject* has *less*. Thus it is in general meant to be understood that in a universal affirmative proposition the *predicate* is wholly united to the subject in the relation of *comprehension*, but not in that of *extension*. Here the word *comprehension* means the *definition of the term*, as in the example given above, it includes all that is meant by the term *incorruptible;* and the word *extension* signifies all the things to which it may be applied. Hence comes the saying that *comprehension* and *extension* stand in inverse ratios to each other, so that as one increases the other diminishes; thus *being* having least comprehension and greatest extension is *transcendental*. The other term is called the *middle* term because, generally speaking, its extension is less

than that of the *major* and greater than that of the *minor*.

3. That proposition which contains the major term is called the *major premiss*, and that which contains the minor the *minor premiss*, though often the one which comes first in speaking or writing is incorrectly called so.

4. In the *major premiss* the major term is compared with the middle term, and its identity (*propositione affirmativa*), or discrepancy (*propositione negativa*), with it expressed. In the *minor premiss* the same comparison is made between the minor and middle terms; and the *conclusion* gives the result of these comparisons and the identity or discrepancy that has been declared, uniting or separating the two extreme terms, as the preceding example has made clear.

When the conclusion of a syllogism will be true.—In order that a *syllogism* may yield a true *conclusion* it should be the expression of the principle of contradiction, which is the first, most certain, and most evident principle. This is thus logically expressed by Aristotle:* *It is absurd that the same predicate under the same relation should be attributed and not attributed to the same subject.* Now if the syllogism is affirmative, it is implicitly affirmed in the two first propositions or in the premisses, that the predicate which is the *major term* belongs to the subject, which is the *minor term*, and, if the syllogism is correctly made, the same thing is explicitly repeated in the conclusion. Therefore if the conclusion were erro-

* IV. Metaph. 9.

neous the principle of contradiction would itself be false, which is impossible. But if the syllogism is negative, then in the premisses the predicate, which is the *major term*, is implicitly denied of the subject, which is the *minor term*, and this is what is explicitly denied in the conclusion, which therefore cannot be erroneous.

The following also are often laid down as principles regulating the syllogism. (*a*) *Dictum de omni, dictum de nullo ;* or, *what is affirmed of all must be affirmed of each, and what is denied of all must be denied of each;* and (*b*) *two things which are equal to a third are equal to each other, and two things are unlike each other if one agrees with a third thing and the other does not.* These principles are excellent (especially the first), inasmuch as they rest upon or express the principle of contradiction ; but to avoid prolixity it will be enough for us to observe that the first part of them governs *affirmative* and the second *negative* syllogisms.

How we can be sure that the syllogism is a genuine expression of the principle of contradiction.—We are so when it is drawn up in the correct *figure* and *mode*. Here we ought to say that Aristotle has with great ingenuity and consummate correctness considered in his *Logic* all possible manners of reasoning, and separated the good from the bad ones. He defines, in the first place, *that every new truth must be the comparison of two simple "verba mentalia" with a third, which is done in two judgments, and they have the power, called consequence, of producing a third judgment, which is called the illation, conclusion, or con-*

sequence. He reckoned sixty-four of these different possible combinations, but among them only fourteen. that were good. Therefore calling the oral expression of the act of reasoning a syllogism, he said that there were only fourteen correct forms of the syllogism by which a proposition not before known could be obtained. He distinguished in the syllogism between the *figure* and the *mode*, and counted only *three* figures under which he distributed the *fourteen* modes. If then our syllogism is made in conformity with one of these figures and modes, we are certain that it is an expression of the principle of contradiction, and this can easily be tested by analyzing it. In the philosophical works of the Stagirite we have a treasure of true knowledge, but if he had even left us nothing but his *Logic* he would still have deserved Dante's splendid eulogium :

> Then when a little more I raised my brow,
> I spied the master of the sapient throng,
> Seated amid the philosophic train
> Him all admire, all pay him reverence due ;
> There Socrates and Plato both I marked
> Nearest to him in rank.*

How figure and mode are defined, and how they are divided.—The *figure* is "the position of the middle term in relation to the two extreme terms in the premisses." The *mode* is "the combination of the quantity and quality in the proposition."

There are three figures. In the first, which is the

---

* *Inf.* iv.

best, the *middle term* forms the *subject* of the *major* *premiss* and the *predicate* of the *minor:* and this figure is divided into four modes which uses the letters as signs which indicate the *quality* and *quantity*, and can be thus expressed:

Maj. A — E — A — E
Min. A — A — I — I
Conc. A — E — I — O

2. The second figure is less perfect than the preceding ; in it the middle term is the *predicate* in both *premisses*—it has four modes:

Maj. E — A — E — A
Min. A — E — I — O
Conc. E — E — O — O

3. In the third, the middle term is the *subject* in both premisses—it has six modes :

Maj. A — E — I — A — O — E
Min. A — A — A — I — A — I
Conc. I — O — I — I — O — O

These fourteen legitimate modes of reasoning will be more easily remembered if we choose a word of three vowels to signify each of them, in which the first vowel indicates the *major*, the second the *minor*, and the third the *conclusion*.

Fig. 1. Malaga, Benares, Assisi, Treviso.

Fig. 2. Belgrade, Manchester, Messico, Marocco.

Fig. 3. Trapani, Bergamo, Chiari, Aiti, Otago, Trebizond.

In the Appendix we will explain why we reject the words anciently used and employ unusual ones.

If to every conclusion we apply the rule for the *conversion* of propositions (Lecture vii. 3) we can obtain from every figure *indirect* conclusions. In order to syllogize correctly it is certainly enough if we arrange the syllogism in such a way that it falls under some mode of one of the given figures. Still we can give eight rules, the observation of which will perfectly ensure the correctness of the syllogism, and that it will be the expression of the principle of contradiction, and will come under some mode of these figures. And if any of these rules are violated the syllogism will not express the principle of contradiction and will lead to error ; or if it does lead to a true conclusion, this will not be in virtue of its construction, but it will be, so to speak, *per accidens.*

1. In a *syllogism* there should be only three terms : the *major, minor*, and *middle term.*

2. There should be nothing in the *conclusion (or effect)* which is not contained in the *premisses (or cause).*

3. The *middle term* must not appear in the *conclusion*, either wholly or in part.

4. The *middle term* should be *universal* either once or twice : the *singular* and the *universal* are equivalent.

5. No conclusion can be drawn from two *negative propositions.*

6. *And none from two particular propositions.*

7. A *negative* conclusion cannot be drawn from two *affirmatives.*

8. If one *premiss* is negative the *conclusion* will also be so, and equally if one premiss is *particular* the conclusion will be *particular.* These are the eight rules.

––––––––––

APPENDIX TO LECTURE VIII.

It is very useful for learners to practise themselves in the composition of syllogisms made according to the rules which we have indicated ; so we give here an example of each figure and mode.

Figure 1. Mode 1. Malaga. Every corporeal substance has in itself quantity and force.'

But every atom is a corporeal substance.

Therefore every atom has in itself quantity and force.

2. Benares. Nothing that has extension is indivisible.

But everything that has length has extension.

Therefore nothing that has length is indivisible.

3. Assisi. Every plant is a living being.

But some insensitive substance is a plant.

Therefore some insensitive substance is living being.

4. Treviso. No immaterial substance is mortal.

But some souls are immaterial substance.

Therefore some souls are not mortal.

Figure 2. Mode 1. Belgrade. No undivided substance is divided within itself.

But every aggregate of atoms is divided within itself.

Therefore no aggregate of atoms is an individual substance.

2. Manchester. Every substance which has a sensitive soul, feels.

But no plant feels.

Therefore no plant has a sensitive soul.

3. Messico. No simple essence is mutable in its nature.

But some substance is mutable in its nature.

Therefore some substance is not simple essence.

4. Marocco. Every physical compound is divisible.

But some substance is not divisible.

Therefore some substance is not a physical compound.

Figure 3. Mode 1. Trapani. Every good physician is a useful citizen.

But every good physician is a learned man.

Therefore some learned men are useful citizens.

2. Bergamo. No immoral theatre is good for the country.

But every immoral theatre is proscribed by the laws.

Therefore some thing which is proscribed by the laws is not good for the country.

3. Chiari. Some citizens are rich.

But all citizens ought to aim at the good of their country.

Therefore some people who ought to aim at the good of their country are rich.

4. Aiti. Every pious man is estimable.

But some pious men are poor.

Therefore some poor men are estimable.

5. Otago. Some Italians do not value the true glory of their ancestors.

But all Italians are Europeans.

Therefore some Europeans do not value the true glory of their ancestors.

6. Trebizond. No virtuous man is avaricious.

But some virtuous men are rich.

Therefore some rich men are not avaricious.

As, however, syllogisms constructed according to the second and third figures are less perfect than those made according to the first, the art was discovered of what is called reducing them to the first. The ancients with great patience invented certain outlandish words which were so contrived as to indicate both the various modes of the syllogism, and at the same time the rules for its reduction. But in our judgment this reduction is of no value, and we have therefore substituted the names of certain cities for these strange words.

And now we wish to warn young people not to allow themselves to be misled by those who disparage the syllogism, as though without it there were other ways of seeking and obtaining truth and defending and demonstrating it. It is true that the syllogism may be expressed in a rhetorical manner, or in any of the various manners which we shall give in the following Lecture; but still it will always remain a syllogism. The question is sometimes asked, What have *induction* and *analogy* to do with the syllogism? and yet they are the most efficacious means for discovering hidden truths, especially in the physical sciences. But we say that all the force of *induction* and *analogy* lies in the *syllogism*, and that both must be reduced to it.

In effect what is *induction? It is a way of reasoning which proceeds from the enumeration of the parts to the whole, or from singulars to the universal.* It is *perfect* if all the parts, or all the singulars, are named; *imperfect,* if only some. In either case it is nothing but a syllogism. Let us suppose a perfect example. I wish to prove that all the planets receive their light from the sun. Proceeding to the whole from the enumeration of singulars, I shall say: The planet A, the planet B (here each one should be named), receive their light from the sun. But all the planets may be reduced to the planet A, the planet B, &c. Therefore all the planets receive their light from the sun. This is a syllogism.

Supposing the induction to be *imperfect,* still all its force lies in the syllogism. I wish to prove that gravity has its source in the nature of bodies. It will not be necessary to have experience of all individual bodies; but having experience of several which are in *various accidental circumstances,* extrinsic and intrinsic, I shall reason thus: That mode of activity which cannot be attributed to accidental causes, extrinsic or intrinsic, must be derived from the nature of the thing; but the gravitation of bodies is a mode of acting which cannot be attributed to accidental causes either extrinsic or intrinsic: therefore the gravitation of bodies has its source in their nature. And is not this a syllogism? Therefore in disparaging the syllogism *induction* also is disparaged.

E

And precisely the same is true of *analogy*, which is a method of reasoning resting wholly on parity and similitude, and is logically nothing but an imperfect induction.

———

LECTURE IX.—THE ART OF FINDING THE MIDDLE TERM. DIVISIONS OF THE SYLLOGISM. SOPHISTRY.

The art of finding the middle term.—The syllogism may be safely used to demonstrate any one of the propositions A, E, I, O, because the singular term is *logically* equivalent to A or to E. The reason of this is that both *universal* and *singular* terms are taken in their whole extension. Thus, when I say, *Every man has reason*, there is not one of the subject *man* who is not here included; and equally when I say, *Dante Alighieri is a sublime poet*, I include here all and only that which is meant by the words *Dante Alighieri.*

(*a*) If we have to demonstrate A, the middle term will be that which is the consequent of the subject and the antecedent of the predicate. For example, to demonstrate: *Every virtue is amiable*—the middle term will be *good*, for it applies to the subject virtue as a *consequent;* thus, *it is a virtue, therefore it is good.* And *good* is the antecedent of the predicate, for we say rightly *it is good; therefore it is amiable.* So we shall make our syllogism thus: *All that is good is amiable; but every virtue is good: therefore every virtue is amiable*, and it will belong to Malaga; or the first mode of the first figure.

(*b*) If the proposition we wish to demonstrate is E, there may be either of two middle terms. (1) If we take the *consequent* of the subject, and that which cannot stand with the predicate or which *disagrees with the predicate*, we may make the syllogism in Benares, the second mode of the first figure; for example, to demonstrate : *no human soul is mortal :* we take *spiritual* for the middle term, which agrees with the human soul and disagrees with mortal, and we say : *No spiritual soul is mortal ; but every human soul is spiritual : therefore no human soul is mortal.* It may equally be made in Belgrade the first mode of the second figure. *No law ought to be despised ; every unjust precept is despicable : therefore no unjust precept is a law.* (2) If we take that which disagrees with the subject and agrees with the predicate of the conclusion E, we shall have a correct middle term under Manchester, the second mode of the second figure. *Every idle man is addicted to vice ; but no praiseworthy man is addicted to vice : therefore no praiseworthy man is idle.*

(*c*) If I is to be demonstrated, the middle term will disagree with the subject and be the antecedent to the predicate, and thus the syllogism will come under Assisi, the third mode of the first figure. I want to prove the conclusion, *Such a religion is false.* I take for the middle term : *it contains precepts which are contrary to the natural law*, which disagrees with the subject and is an antecedent to the predicate, and I shall have a correct syllogism. It is unnecessary to dwell upon the middle terms for the first, third, and fourth modes of the third figure, which are of little value.

(*d*) If I wish to demonstrate O, the middle term will be the antecedent of the subject and the contrary of the predicate; such is the middle term of the following syllogism in Treviso: *No sacrilegious robber can enjoy a lasting prosperity; but that rich man is a sacrilegious robber: therefore that rich man cannot enjoy lasting prosperity.* Here also it is unnecessary to seek for the middle term for the third and fourth mode of the second figure, or the second, fifth, and sixth of the third.

How syllogisms are divided.—They are divided into *simple* and *compound*. *The simple is one which is made of simple propositions; the compound of compound ones.*

(*a*) The *simple* syllogism is divided into *the categorical*, of which we have already spoken and given several examples.

(2) The *enthymeme*, which is now called a *categorical* syllogism, in which one of the two premisses is suppressed. Aristotle gave the name of enthymeme to a syllogism, which deduced the probable illation from probable premisses, precisely following the second rule of the syllogism.

(3) The *sorites*, which is an orderly series of categorical syllogisms. It is so arranged that the predicate of the first proposition is the subject of the second; the predicate of the second goes on to be the subject of the third, and so on until it arrives at a conclusion, which is formed of the *subject* of the

first and the *predicate* of the last. For example: *God is a necessary being ; a necessary being is a perfect being; a perfect being is an omnipotent being; an omnipotent being can do everything that does not involve a contradiction: therefore God can do everything that does not involve a contradiction.* This proposition is rightly made if all the propositions in it except two are found conformable to the rule above given. It should also be noted that for this to be the case, first, the *predicate* of the antecedent proposition should become the *subject* of the following one without any alteration ; secondly, no proposition except the first should be particular, and if that is particular the *conclusion* must also be so; thirdly, there may be one *negative* before the conclusion, but it must immediately precede it, and the conclusion then will also be *negative.*

(4) The *polysyllogism*, which is a *categorical* syllogism to which another *categorical* is added, the first premiss of which is the conclusion of the preceding one. For example: *God is the Author of the true religion; but the Christian religion is the religion of which God is the Author: therefore the Christian religion is the true religion. But we are bound to embrace the true religion: therefore we are bound to embrace the Christian religion.*

(*b*) The compound syllogism is divided into (1) copulative syllogisms, where there is some copulative proposition. To be true, it requires (besides the ordinary rules) that the copulative propositions should be true. For example: *Whoever is endowed with sense and reason, though mortal, has an immortal soul;*

but man is endowed with sense and reason : therefore man, though mortal, has an immortal soul. Here ·modern philosophers frequently give examples which do not *really* belong to the *copulative*, but to the disjunctive syllogism, as would be this one : *No one can serve God and mammon ; but many do serve mammon : therefore many do not serve God.*

2. *Distributive* syllogisms, where the major is distributive. The conclusion is good (1) when there are two things denied or affirmed in the major, and it denies or affirms one of them ; as, *Thou art either a true or a false friend ;* but thou art *not a true friend : therefore thou art a false friend ;* (2) when the major, having more than two members, one is denied in the minor, and all the others are affirmed, but *distributively*, in the *conclusion*, or one being affirmed in the minor, all the others are absolutely denied in the *conclusion ;* (3) it is necessary that the distribution should be adequate, that is, that there shall be no other members that might be enumerated.

3. *Conditional*, where the major is conditional. To be correct : (1) It must affirm the condition in the minor, and thence the thing conditioned in the conclusion ; or (2) it must deny the thing conditioned in the minor and the condition in the conclusion, thus : *If you are silent you acknowledge it ; but you are silent, therefore you acknowledge it. If oxygen and hydrogen were of like nature they would produce like effects ; but they do not produce like effects : therefore they are not of like nature.*

4. *Causal* (epichirema) where the reason of the union of the predicate with the subject is indicated in

one premiss. To make this syllogism good the reason must be *true*.

5. *Discrete* (dilemma), which is also called a horned syllogism, because the distributive major is formed of two members opposed to each other in such a manner that, if either is admitted, whoever denies the proposition must be beaten. But be careful that the conclusion cannot be turned against you. This would be an excellent dilemma to oppose to one who punished any without trial : *Those that you punish are either innocent or guilty; if they are innocent you are committing a crime; if they are guilty, why do you forbid that they should be tried?* On the contrary, if any one excused himself for not exerting himself in the cause of his country by saying, *I must remain alone and inactive; for if I do anything for my country it will either be for its true good or the reverse; if what I do is for its true good, I shall have the whole tribe of evil-doers against me ; if not, I shall incur the anger of the good :* to which it may be retorted, *You ought to labour for your country; for if you labour for its true good you will have the approbation of the good; if the contrary, you will have the praise of the bad.*

This will suffice for the different kinds of syllogisms.

The demonstration ad absurdum.—It is that by which an opponent who disputes a true and legitimate conclusion is forced either to admit it or to deny the principle of contradiction.

The forms of the first figure are so self-evident that it would be impossible for an opponent to deny them, but to deny the conclusion of the second and third figure is a conceivable audacity. In case then (1) the conclusion of the second figure is denied, we shall retain the *major*, but for the minor we substitute the contradictory of the conclusion, which our opponent cannot deny, for of two contradictories one must be true; then we draw our conclusion, which will be the contradictory of a proposition which our opponent has admitted, but he cannot deny it, for it is drawn in the most evident mode of the first figure. For example: you have made the syllogism, *No stone is a living being; but every man is a living being: therefore, no man is a stone.* Your opponent denies the conclusion, and according to this rule you say, *No stone is a living being; some men are stones, therefore some men are not living beings.* And thus your opponent is forced to deny the principle of contradiction, for he is obliged to admit that a man both is and is not a living being.

2. If the conclusion of a syllogism made according to the third figure is denied, he will be brought to the same point by substituting the contradictory of the conclusion for the major, and retaining the minor. The result will be a syllogism in the first figure, with a contrary conclusion to that which your opponent has already conceded.

Sophisms, and how they are divided.—A sophism is "a syllogism which appears to be regular but is not so really." It always violates some one of the rules which we have given, but surreptitiously, with intent to deceive.

Sophisms are divided into (1) *Logical Sophisms*, (2) *Material Sophisms.*

1. Logical sophisms are (*a*) *Amphibology*, when a word having two meanings is used, with a different one in each premiss, thus making really *four* terms in the syllogism, though there seem to be only three, and a false conclusion follows, thus: *Anger is a passion; but God is angry; therefore God has passions.* In the major anger is understood as it is in man, in whom it is a real emotion, prompting to revenge ; in the minor it is taken *analogically*, as it is in God, in whom it is not an emotion, and who is only called angry in *a figure* because He punishes the guilty. The way to unmask this is to distinguish the meanings in the premisses.

(*b*) Sophisms of *composition*, or, conversely, of *division*, where the equivocation consists in insinuating that the terms should be used *collectively* or *distributively;* for example : *It is impossible that any one who sleeps should be awake; but Peter sleeps: therefore it is impossible that he should be awake.* Here the major is to be admitted in a collective sense, *i.e.*, *with sleep*, but denied in a *distributive* sense, *i.e.*, when not sleeping. Or, *You bought raw meat; but you ate what you bought, therefore you ate raw meat.* Here the minor taken in a *collective* sense is denied, in a *distributive* sense it is admitted.

(*c*) *The sophism of treating a particular meaning as though it were universal;* thus : *A learned man is estimable; but this impious man is learned: therefore he is estimable.* Here we must *distinguish:* if in the major the meaning is *particular, in so far as he is learned*, we admit it ; if the meaning is *universal*, we deny it.

(*d*) The sophism of confounding affirmation with exclusion, for example : *Your aim should be to live well; therefore you should not occupy yourself with the study of philosophy.* Here I distinguish the antecedent : among other things, *I grant*, only, *I deny.*

2. *Material Sophisms are—*

(*a*) *The ignoratio elenchi*, when the question is evaded by tacitly ignoring it ; and this often happens when a person finding himself incapable of discerning the subject in hand, changes the question without the other perceiving it.

(*b*) *The vicious circle*, when, under a cloud of words to conceal the device, a person proves one thing by means of another, and that other by the first.

(*c*) *The petitio principii*, when to prove one thing another which is still more questionable is supposed true.

(*d*) *The false cause*, when a thing which is only an antecedent is adduced as though it were a cause, according to the old sophistical adage, *Post hoc, ergo ex hoc*, though it is only a concomitant. Writers on jurisprudence and physical and medical scientists are very apt to fall into this kind of sophistry.

(*e*) *Invalid inductions*, when a universal conclusion is drawn from the enumeration of a few non-essential particulars. Historians and young people often fall into this.

Finally, any one who reflects upon the definitions of *sophisms* will see that (*a*) an excessive opinion of oneself, (*b*) a weak reliance on the authority of others, (*c*) the disturbance of various passions, &c., may be called incentives to error, but are not the source of *sophistry* as some people say.

APPENDIX TO LECTURE IX.

We have given in the Lecture the general way of discovering the middle term, but philosophers, and still more orators, will wish to know the sources from which the terms themselves can be most easily obtained, that they may use them either in concise syllogisms or in more diffuse arguments and illustrations. We think it well here, therefore, to borrow a little from Lully's famous method, which was specially designed to supply these sources. Take this table :

Absolute Predicates	Goodness Intelligence	Greatness Wisdom	Duration Truth	Power Virtue	Felicity
Relative Predicate	Difference Middle	Conformity End	Opposition Greater	Principle, Equal	Less
Questions	If? How much?	What? Which?	Of what? When?	Wherefore? Where?	How? With what?
Subjects	God Animal	Angel Plant	Man Mineral	Heaven Accident	Instrument

There are two things to be observed in this table. (1) That every *abstract* term includes also its *concrete*, its *like*, and its *kind*; for example, *goodness, good, to benefit, a benefit, &c.*, and (2) all the many answers to each interrogation or question; for example, If ?—if it exists, if it acts, if it suffers. What ?—what it is in itself, in others, absolutely, relatively. This being understood, it will be seen that all thinkable things may be reduced to some one of the words indicated in this table; and thus it will be found a complete compendium of middle terms.

Now express in a clear conclusion either affirmative or negative, the thing which you intend to treat of, then search among the subjects for the one to which it belongs, combine it with predicates absolute and relative, and co-ordinate it with the questions indicated; for example, if you want to demonstrate *that we should love our country*, the subject will be *accident* because love is an accident.

You will find plenty of predicates in the first line. The love of country is a *good*; so we have: (1) The love of country is beneficial both for individuals and families. (2) Love of one's country gives true *greatness*, it is noble, it is estimable. (3) When infused into the heart it *endures* through the whole of life, its beneficial effects extend to the most remote generations. (4) He who truly loves his county becomes *powerful*, because he is supported by all, &c., and when citizens love their country they make it *strong* against its enemies. And what has been done with each of these words in the first line can also be done in all the following ones, and thus an abundance of middle terms can be found for use in discoursing on the question that has been chosen.

But let no one think that this art will take the place of knowledge. "Cui lecta potenter erit res, nec facundia deseret hunc nec lucidus ordo," says Horace. It is necessary to take pains and be well acquainted with the subject of which you mean to treat. This device of Lully's (and it is the same with all others) is only a useful means of arousing the mind and recalling points which would otherwise not have occurred to it. And for this reason this art is especially serviceable to beginners.

THE FOURTH PART.

LECTURE X.—THE FINAL CAUSE OF THE RATIONAL
ORDER. TRUTH AND KNOWLEDGE.

*The final cause of the rational order is the end to which
it is directed,* and this *end* is called a *cause,* because
without it the rational order would have no reason
for existing. This end is the apprehension of truth,
which is obtained in three ways—(1) by *knowledge;*
(2) by *experience;* (3) by *faith.*

What *truth* is.

Truth is *the abstract of the true,* or *that by which
the true is called true.* Now the true is *being as known
by the intellect.* Truth, then, consists in the knowledge
of the intellect, which proceeds from a conformity or
equivalence with the thing known; it may therefore
be defined as *the equivalence between the intellect and
the thing known:* adæquatio rei et intellectus. This
is truth properly so called, and is also transferred to
things in so far as they are capable of generating in
the mind a true knowledge of themselves (hence the
equivalence just mentioned). Thus we say *true gold,* a
true friend, &c., because these things present themselves to the reason in such a manner that they can
be recognized in the definition of gold, of a friend, &c.
Contrariwise brass, a flatterer, are called false gold,
a false friend, because they generate a false cognition,
or a cognition in which there *is not equivalence* or
conformity between the knowledge and the thing
known.

Every truth is mentally expressed in a complex word or judgment and signified in a proposition, which is therefore said to be *true*, and which is said to be *false* if it is not the sign of a judgment in which truth is expressed. And, as we said, a proposition is true when the connection or separation which it indicates between the subject and predicate is real, and false when it is not. Thus this proposition is true : *Man is by nature formed for society;* and the reverse is false : *Man is not by nature formed for society.*

From this it is manifest that the end of logic may be said to be to dispose the intellect towards the apprehension of truth, or the knowledge of things as they really are.

What knowledge is.—Knowledge is a "certain and evident cognition of the causes of the things known." Let us examine this definition in detail.

1. We say it is a *cognition.* It would be a useless prolixity here to treat of intellectual cognition, which will be fully discussed elsewhere when we come to the philosophy of man. Those elementary notions will suffice for the present which we gave in the beginning, and from which we learnt that cognition consists in a complex word of the mind, or a judgment signified by a proposition and produced by the intellect informed of the intelligible species of things.

2. *Certain* is equivalent to firm, stable, determined. Knowledge is called certain because of the certainty of the information which produces it, and which therefore causes this firmness, stability, and determinateness in the intellectual cognition. It is the opposite

of *doubt*, which is a balancing and oscillation of the intellect between "yes" and "no," and of *opinion*, which is an unstable cognition, or one that is not firm. Thus the cognitions signified by the propositions: *The whole is greater than its part; The sun gives light; Constantinople exists;* are firm and therefore *certain.* On the other hand, the mind of a physician is often in doubt, vacillating between two mental words: *This morbid state proceeds from inflammation,* or, *It has been caused by some deleterious food.* And perhaps he determines on the first judgment, but still not with true firmness, but only *opining.* From this we see that certainty contains two elements —one positive, the other negative; the positive is *stability,* and thus can increase; the negative is *non-anticipation of the opposite,* and this belongs to *things indivisible.* Further on we shall formulate the *cause* of certainty. At present it is enough to note only one general division of certainty, namely, that of *subjective* and *objective.* The first is personal, and is that *firmness in cognition* which has been already described; the second is extra-personal, and is the *capability residing in the object of being known with this firmness.*

3. *Evident.* I will employ an example to make the force of this word intelligible in this treatise. Suppose before your eyes a lighted candle. You say at once: *I see it.* It is *evident* to you that there is a candle alight because *it is present to you.* Thus in the dark I say to you: Observe this picture. You say, *I do not see it.* But when you bring a candle you say, *I see it,* and it is *evident* to you that the

picture is there because it is present. The *mode* in which the thing so clearly manifests its presence to you is its visibility, or its evidence. Premising this with regard to vision, from whence the name *evidence* is taken, we transfer its application to the order of cognitions. Here is a cognition expressed in its sign, that is, in a proposition : *The whole is greater than its part.* Does the eye of the mind see its truth, or the nexus between the subject and predicate ? It does see it, and it sees it the moment it apprehends the terms. Therefore this truth is present to the eye of the mind as the lighted candle to the eye of the body; and this *mode* by which the truth manifests its presence to you is *evidence.* Now, if I say to any one who does not know geometry, *The square of the hypotenuse is equal to the sum of the squares of its sides,* even when he understands the terms and knows what the square of the hypotenuse and the squares of the sides mean, he will not at once see the connection between the predicate and the subject; the truth will not be present to him immediately, but will require to be accurately demonstrated before he can say *I see it,* as you saw the picture when you brought the lighted candle. Therefore in the first case the evidence is *immediate,* in the second *mediate.* At the same time, though evidence belongs to the object *in so far as it shows itself clearly present to the subject,* and is therefore properly *objective,* yet it is also indirectly called *subjective,* in so far as the subject apprehends the object which thus manifests its presence.

In order to make our meaning as clear as possible,

F

we have cited *propositions,* and have said that when
the terms are apprehended the eye of the mind sees
the truth. But as we said before, the terms are the
signs of *the things* known, and the proposition is *the
sign, with the judgment as its medium, of the real
existence of the things;* therefore, strictly speaking,
objective evidence is the existence or *being* of the thing
itself in so far as it is an object, that is, in so far as it
presents itself to (objicitur) the intellect.

Faith is the opposite of *evidence,* so that the great
St. Augustine said : Quid est fides ? Credere quod
non vides. So if I propound this proposition, *God is
one Essence and three Persons,* and ask, do you *see* the
"nexus" between the predicate and the subject ? or
do you see its truth ? you reply, no ! and whatever
demonstrations I may attempt, you will never say,
I see it. This shows that this is a truth which is not
evident or visible to the intellect either *mediately* or
immediately, but is accepted and believed on the
motive of Divine authority.

4. We said, finally, *of the causes of the things known.*
These words can be taken in a twofold sense. In
the first place we must observe that there are four
causes : *efficient, material, formal, final.* Now when
a thing is capable of having all these four causes, in
order to have a scientific knowledge of it, it is necessary that all these causes should be known ; for
scientific knowledge should be complete. In the
second place, we observe that in every cognition the
predicate is applied to the subject. Now it may be
asked (1) For what cause is the predicate *applied* to
this subject ? (2) For what cause does this subject

require this predicate? And it is the knowledge of this second cause which is necessary for science; the first is not enough. Thus if I say, *Pekin is a very large city*, although I know the motive (authority) upon which, believing it, I apply the predicate to the subject, still I have not that knowledge of the cause which is requisite for science. But if I say, *The human soul is immortal*, and I know the cause for which this subject *requires* this predicate—for example, because it is spiritual—in this case I have the knowledge of that cause which is necessary for a scientific cognition of things.

It is true that this word knowledge may be used to signify any cognition; but as we have wished to indicate that which is most perfect, and which entirely satisfies the intellect, which tends to embrace truth as far as it can immediately, it is right for us to retain this definition, which has been unanimously employed by philosophers for so many centuries, and which we have given and explained.

LECTURE XI.—EXPERIENCE AND FAITH. THE FORMAL OBJECTS OF CERTAINTY.

Experience.—*Experience is the perception of a thing by any cognitive faculty, not through the medium of intelligible or sensible species, but immediately.* This definition shows the difference between knowledge and experience; for in knowledge the object is ideal, in experience it is the thing itself. For example, when I say, *The whole is greater than a part*, my judgment is determined by the ideal essence of *the whole*, which is reflected in and illuminates my mind, and therefore my judgment is *universal*, that is, applicable to all those things in which the idea of the whole is expressed; therefore to every man, every plant, every individual of whatever genus or species. But when I say, *The tower of Pisa leans; this iron is hot; I have a severe pain in my foot; I see my brother,* &c.; in forming these judgments my motive is not the ideal essence of the subjects of them, but I judge because I perceive or have perceived the particular things of which I thus judge, and therefore my judgments are not universal.

The divisions of experience.—Experience is divided into *external* and *internal.* This is again divided into *inferior* and *superior*, which last is also called *consciousness. External experience is the perception of bodies and their effects on the external senses; inferior internal experience is the perception by the internal sense of the modifications in our sensations; superior internal experience, the perception of spiritual affections of the soul by the intellectual faculty (direct consciousness), and the reflection on such affections when perceived (reflected consciousness).* It would be out of place here to treat of the various faculties which have just been indicated and the modes in which they experience their objects, since this can only be done with due clearness when we come to treat of anthropology.

*Faith.—*Faith is a *judgment* by which we pronounce *a thing true on the motive of the authority* *of the person who affirms it.* Hence it appears (1) that the subject of faith (potentia quæ *subjicitur fidei*) is not the will but the intellect; (2) that *this judgment* cannot be evident, because the nexus between the subject and the predicate is not manifest either *immediately* or *mediately.* I have said *this judgment,* this, which is called an act of faith or assent to authority, because the same truth may very well be expressed in another judgment which is known by the light of reason, and partakes therefore of evidence. Thus a person may say that *two triangles which have two sides and the angle contained by them equal, are equal,* believing this on the authority of the professor who says so (faith), and afterwards he may affirm the same thing determined by the demonstration by which its truth is shown (knowledge). Therefore the great doctor, Suarez, said, "Fides sumitur pro *cognitione obscura* fundata in testimonio dicentis, quæ in divinam et humanam et etiam angelicam dividetur" (De Fide Disp. i. Sect. i.). Hence, as it is impossible that the same act can have the contradictory characteristics of clearness and obscurity; be determined by the intellect which *sees* its object, and the will which moves the intellect without seeing it to believe; it is also impossible that the *same act relating to the same object* can be at once an act of faith and one of knowledge.

The divisions of faith.—*Faith* is (1) human, when we believe on the authority of a man who affirms some truth (dogmatic faith), or relates some fact (historic faith); (2) Divine, when the authority which we believe is of God.

And here we must observe that *authority is properly that moral force residing in the person who testifies, by which we are led to believe his testimony.* And this force proceeds (*a*) from his *knowledge of the truth,* or acquaintance with the fact which he asserts; (*b*) from his *veraciousness.* This is plain, since the more clearly we see his knowledge of the truth or of the fact, and the more certain we are that he is incapable of a lie, the more inclined we are to give credit to his testimony ; and, conversely, it would be folly to believe an ignorant man, or a liar.

If the man has seen that which he relates, or himself knows or has experienced it, his testimony is called *ocular;* if he has received it from another it is called *aural.*

The formal object of certainty and its divisions.— In our cognitions or mental judgments we must distinguish (*a*) the thing which is known from (*b*) the motive which constrains the intellect and determines it to pronounce a judgment. The thing which is known is called the *material object;* the motive which determines the intellect, on which, as we have seen, certainty depends, is called the *formal object.* But what is that which determines the intellect to judge ?

1. If the knowledge is (*a*) concerning analytic judgments, the truth of which shines by immediate evidence, then that which determines my intellect to pronounce them is the nexus between the subject and the predicate immediately manifest. Thus I am instantly determined to judge that *the whole is greater than its part,* because the nexus between the whole and the part presents itself to me with imme-

diate evidence ; (*b*) if it concerns analytic judgments whose truth is not immediately evident, it will still be the nexus between the predicate and the subject that will determine me, but it will present itself to me in the premisses of the demonstration which makes the conclusion *mediately* manifest and evident. I have said that the nexus which evidently presents itself to me determines my intellect, in order to denote that the *truth itself,* not the mode (evidence) in which it presents itself to me, is the formal object of scientific cognition, although sometimes the name evidence is given to the actual truth which so presents itself. Thus Aquinas says, " *Certitudo, quæ est in scientia* (concerning deductive judgments), *et in intellectu* (concerning immediate judgments), *est ex ipsa evidentia eorum quæ certa esse dicuntur* " (Sent. i. Dist. iii. Quæst. 2, Art. 2).

2. In *experimental cognition,* what determines the intellect is not, as in knowledge, the *truth* of things expressed in judgments and signified in analytical propositions, but the fact itself presented to and united with the cognitive faculty. Thus, what determines my intellect to pronounce the judgment, *I feel pain,* is the pain itself, actually present. So that in experimental cognition the *formal object* is the *fact itself* manifestly present to the intellect. To examine *how* it manifests itself belongs to another place.

3. In *faith* it is neither the *truth* manifesting itself by *immediate* or *mediate evidence,* nor the fact presenting itself to the mind, but *authority* which inclines the intellect to embrace that which is asserted, or to *believe* the person who bears testimony, and this

authority, made up of the knowledge and the veracity of the attestor, is the *formal object* of certainty. Now since the intellect is a power whose acts are necessary and not free, it will not be necessarily determined to produce a *word* or *judgment* concerning a thing, unless it is moved by a truth manifesting itself *immediately* or *mediately* to it in the ideal order, as is the case in *knowledge*, or by the presence of the thing, as in *experience*. But authority does not present the truth to it as *evident*, either *immediately* or *mediately*, nor yet the thing itself; but it shows it the *extrinsic* reasonableness of believing it. Hence it is necessary that the will, which has dominion over the other powers of man, and often determines their acts, should determine the intellect to pronounce a judgment, or to believe. Therefore *the act of believing is free*, in so far as the will which governs the intellect concurs in producing it. And the empire exercised by the will over the powers which are under it is so strong that sometimes it determines them to an act with greater intensity than when they are determined by their own natural objects, and thus the will can *determine* the intellect to believe, and make it much more *fixed* and *stable* in its act of faith than it is when moved by a truth or a fact which it sees, so that sometimes the *certainty of faith* may be more stable than the *certainty of experience* or *knowledge*.

In our designation of the formal objects, it may be thought that in what concerns *knowledge* and *experience* we have really taught that the *formal* and the *material object* are the same, when we said that the formal object of knowledge is *truth manifest to us in the ideal order*, and that of experience the *fact itself present.* But any discriminating person will easily see that there is a distinction between *truth* and *this truth*, between the *fact present* and *this fact*, and that the *motive* is not the truth or fact as *this* or *that*, but simply as *truth and fact manifest to the cognitive faculty.* It is the same in vision, where the formal object is colour, and the material this or that definite colour.

Finally, let us remark that the *certainty* produced by the *formal object of knowledge* is called *metaphysical*, because it springs immediately from the ideal order; the certainty produced by the *formal object of experience* is called *physical*, because it comes from the physical order; that produced by *authority* is *moral*, because it rests *specially* on the veracity of witnesses who, by the laws which regulate manners (*mores*, whence *moral*), are bound to be truthful. I say specially, because any one who, being defective in knowledge, bore testimony to that of which he was ignorant, would almost always be wanting in veracity.

LECTURE XII.—THE CRITERION OF TRUTH.

The criterion of truth.—All philosophers, and more particularly those of the last hundred years, have treated of the criterion of truth; but very few have troubled themselves to give a plain definition of it, and in consequence they have lost themselves in innumerable controversies, and obscured that which, as they taught, so shone by its own light that no one was ever able to gainsay it. Some have taken the criterion of truth to be the *motive* which *determines* the intellect in its judgments, or the *formal object* of certainty; others calling it *evidence* or *clearness* in the *cognitive faculty*, had placed it in the *mode* by which the object presents itself; others holding it to be *human reason*, have confounded it with the *cognitive faculty*, or calling it the *light of the general reason*, have considered it as an *intellectual force*. But it would take many lectures to describe and examine all these different opinions, and they would not be of the least use to beginners; we will therefore leave them and define the *criterion of truth*.

The *criterion of truth* is the rule *according to which the intellect ought to judge of all things*. Hence (1). As the thing regulated cannot be deduced from the rule, for example, as from the idea of order the existence of the things that are ordered cannot be inferred, or as from the existence of a measure we cannot infer the existence of the thing that it can measure; so the judgments themselves cannot be deduced from the criterion of truth, by which I am to measure the truth of my judgments. (2) As in some sense the rule exists in the thing regulated, so the *criterion of truth* should exist in all true judgments. (3) That judgment which is not regulated by, or does not express, the rule which it ought to express, will be perverse, faulty, bad; and that which does express it, right, perfect and good; and, therefore, those judgments which do not express their rule or the criterion of truth will be false, and those which do express it will be true. Having established this, we say:

1. The *supreme criterion of truth* is the *divine truth*, or the divine *intellect*, inasmuch as it contains the *primary principles of all truth.* This is the universal criterion for every rational creature, as it is the criterion by which, so to speak, God Himself judges of things. Therefore whatever conforms to this supreme criterion of truth for man, cannot be judged false either by an angel or by God Himself. Every judgment which is opposed to this criterion is *necessarily* false.

2. The criterion of *participated and immediate* truth for man is the *human intellect*, inasmuch as in it are found those *first principles* which are as it were the *laws* which man must observe in order to judge rightly, and which therefore are expressed in such judgments.

The human intellect inasmuch as it contains these first principles may be called the *copy* of the divine, which is the supreme rule of all truth. This is manifest because the (*a*) human intellect bears the impress of God, *signatum est super vos lumen vultus tui, Domine;* and by virtue of this light the human mind becomes the image of the divine mind; and because (*b*) we do not acquire these *first principles* by study or art, but they spring up *naturally* within us (as we shall presently see) in the presence of their objects, so that they must also be said to be impressed on the intellect by God, the Author of nature, and derived from Him as their *Master*, according to the ancient maxim : *in necessariis causa causæ est causa causati.*   But one of these is the principle of contradiction—it is impossible for a thing under the same relation both to be and not to be— this principle is *supremely evident:* it is universal in the highest degree, and is acknowledged by every one; and, as we demonstrate in our Primal Philosophy, its relation is *primary* towards all other principles and judgments.   Therefore we said that the supreme criterion of truth in which man participates, is the human intellect, inasmuch as it presents the *principle of contradiction,* or we may say, it *is the principle of contradiction.*

And now we wish to show that our statement is the same as that of the great Italian philosopher, Aquinas.   Designating the criterion of truth he says : " That truth *according to which* the soul judges of all things is *primary truth* . . . The truth of the first principles *by which* we judge of all things, proceeds from the divine intellect, as its type, into our intellect.   And since it is only inasmuch as it is the image of the primal truth that we can judge by it, we say that we judge *according to primary truth*" (Quæst. 1. De Verit. 4 ad 5).   In the words, *according to which the soul judges of all things,* we have precisely our definition of the *criterion of truth,* and in that which follows is evidently indicated the *supreme* criterion which is God ; and the *participated and immediate* criterion, the *first principles according to* the truth of which we judge of all things.   Else- where he assigns the primacy to the principle of contradiction thus : " There is a certain order in

these things which men learn. Therefore the first
of all things to be learnt is being, the knowledge of
which is included in every conception. And, therefore, the *first indemonstrable principle* is that it is
impossible at the same time to affirm and deny
existence; which principle is founded on the conception of being and not being, and *all the other
principles are founded on this,* as the Philosopher says
in his fourth book on Metaphysics" (1 Part. Quæ.
94. 2).

From these words of Aquinas it is manifest that
the *first* criterion of truth in which we participate
with God, and *by which* we are to pronounce upon
the truth of our judgments, is the *principle of contradiction.* And now let those who, wishing to take
shelter under the authority of St. Thomas, assert that
his doctrine is contrary to ours, pay attention to this,
and not confound the *motive* or *formal object* of
certainty which (Lect. xi.) according to us and to
St. Thomas is *objective truth* or *objective evidence,*
with the rule or the *law* which is the *typal truth* in
all our judgments and is the criterion of which we
have treated. Thus, for example, when contem-
plating certain human actions, I affirm *they are just,*
to have learnt that they are *real* will not be a
sufficient motive, but I must also see in them expressed
that universal judgment concerning justice, which is in
my memory; and equally, for me to be able to say,
this *judgment* is true, I am not sufficiently *determined*
by knowing the thing judged of to be a reality,
but I must see also that my judgment expresses
the primary law of all true judgments, or of primary

truth, which is the principle of contradiction. Our
opponents are right in saying that my judgment
is true because it is in conformity with the reality,
but besides this, I know that it is in such conformity,
and that it is *true* because I see in it fulfilled the
primary law of adjudication, or the criterion of truth,
which is the principle of contradiction.

'Since then (1) according to Aquinas, the light of
human reason is a participation in the increased light
of the Divine mind, and since (2) according to the
same authority, the first principle is learnt by nature,
and therefore our knowledge of it must be ascribed to
God, the Author of nature ; and since (3) this principle
is the germ of all human sciences and cognitions, we
must say that *when man is faithful to the use and
application of this principle he is guided by God Himself,*
and that *properly speaking it is not man but God who
is the master of all the sciences.* How solid then is the
foundation on which rests the edifice of human
philosophy ! "All intelligible things are not in equally
close relation to the cognitive faculty of the intellect,
but some truths are seen by it at once and others not
until after the knowledge of other principles. Hence
there are two sources from which man derives the
knowledge of unknown truths, from the light of the
intellect and from primary truths known in themselves, which are relatively to that light as the instrument to the artificer. And with regard to both these
sources *God* is in a most excellent way the *cause of
human science*; because He adorned the soul with this
intellectual light, and impressed upon it the consciousness of first principles, which are as the seeds of the

sciences, just as in other natural things He impressed the germinal principles (rationes seminales) of all their effects. But since in the order of nature, all men are equal as regards the intellectual light, no man can be the cause of knowledge in another, either producing or increasing the intellectual light in him. For since principles known in themselves are the cause of the knowledge of unknown truths, a man is not the cause of knowledge in another by communicating to him the cognizance of principles, but only by means of sensible signs manifested to the external senses by which truths are called into action which were implicitly and potentially contained in the principles " (De Magistro, Art. 2). From which we see the universality, the truth, and the sublimity of that sentence of Holy Scripture speaking of God : *Qui docet hominem scientiam* (Psalm xciii.). We see that every human science is divinely initiated, and that God is the true (and speaking strictly with Aquinas) the only Teacher of man.

But in enunciating this sublime and immutable criterion of truth there are two warnings that must be given. The first is that the *natural* Divine teaching must never be confounded with supernatural revelation. For revelation gives faith, but natural teaching is not only reconcilable with science, but without it science is impossible. The second is that though we have pointed out this Divine teaching to show how solid is the edifice of human philosophy, still we are able to prescind from God if He is denied, or in the course of the processes of philosophical demonstration, since every man (still setting God aside) must admit

without any demonstration these two things : (1) that
we have the light of reason by which we can pursue
truth, (2) that the primary principle of contradiction
is absolutely true. Neither of these things can be
demonstrated without a *petitio principii*, because in
demonstrating it we are forced to *assume* the light of
reason, which guides us to the truth that we intend to
demonstrate, and we have to *assume* the truth of that
principle of contradiction which, as we saw in treating
of the syllogism, is the *form* of every demonstration.
Hence the sceptic who will have nothing true, and he
who doubts about everything, and from his doubts
thinks he can educe certain cognitions and sciences,
are fools who cannot be brought to reason by the way
of demonstration.

But now it will be well for us to show that, setting
aside God and His Divine governance, the principle
of contradiction is the *universal criterion of truth.* In
fact, what are the properties of the *universal criterion
of truth?* They are (1) that it should be that truth
according to which we ought to judge, so that in
affirming what is true we affirm it, and in denying
what is true we deny it. (2) It should be the most
primary, universal, indemonstrable, self-evident truth,
such that it is impossible to impugn it without conceding it. But these are the properties of the principle
of contradiction. It must be admitted (1) that every
proposition is either *analytic* or *synthetic.* If we
affirm an *analytic* truth, for example, *The whole is
greater than its part*, we affirm that the whole is all ;
if we deny it we deny that the whole is all, and thus
affirm or deny the principle of contradiction. Equally,

if I affirm a *synthetic* proposition, as *Peter is tired*, I affirm fatigue in Peter who is tired, if I deny it I deny fatigue in Peter who is tired, and I affirm or deny the principle of contradiction. (2) That since the principle of contradiction is the most primary, universal, indemonstrable, evident truth, which it is impossibᴊe to impugn without conceding it, it is manifeᴕ that it is the *form* of all correct ratiocination (preceding Lecture), and therefore that in all our discourse we are obliged to assume the truth of this same principle. Its supremacy and universality will be afterwards demonstrated when we speak on Primary Philosophy. But no philosopher denies this property to the principle of contradiction. And if the same properties are attributed to those other principles which modern philosophers give as *universal criterions of truth* it will be evident that they cannot be applied to them. The common fault of the moderns is, as we have pointed out, to confound the *formal objects of certainty* with the *criterion of truth*. They require to be convinced that *that* is not the *criterion of truth* which is necessarily bound up with the possession of it, but that which expresses the law of all our true judgments.

LECTURE XIII.—SCIENTIFIC METHOD.

What is meant by Method?—The word Method signifies the *order or process which should be used in the pursuit of certainty or truth*. This process may

G

be considered under two aspects, where it aims at *certainty and truth concerning a particular matter* and where its aim is the *study of philosophy as a whole, or of the single sciences which are its parts.*

The reason why me say certainty and truth; and why these are not synonymous or necessarily united.— Because, according to the definitions that have been given, *certainty* or the firmness and stability of the intellect in the judgment pronounced is one thing, and the *truth* or conformity or *equivalence* between the cognizing intellect and the thing known is another. *Certainty* and *truth*, however, are necessarily united to each other, but with a variable necessity. *Metaphysical* certainty which resides in *analytic judgments* of immediate or mediate evidence, which are those with which science concerns itself, is united with truth by a *metaphysical necessity* which excludes the contrary. Therefore, it is impossible that *metaphysical certainty* should be false. For example, I am certain that *the whole is greater than its part;* and this judgment is true in such a manner that it is impossible that in any case its predicate should not agree with the subject.

Physical certainty which resides in *synthetic judgment determined by experience* is united to the truth by a physical necessity, which does not exclude the contrary, but where the contrary cannot exist without an exception in those laws by which the world is governed. Thus the son of Tobias was certain that the person with whom he was dealing was a mortal, *and he had no apprehension of the contrary,* although really the person was an angel in a human form.

Moral certainty which resides in *general judgments on the authority of others*, or in acts of faith by which credit is given to God or to men, is united to the truth by a moral necessity. In relation to the Divine authority this necessity is equivalent to the metaphysical, since it is intrinsically impossible that God should be wanting either in knowledge or veracity; but where it is a question of human authority the motives of credibility may sometimes be far from trivial, and the will may determine the intellect and the act of faith, when afterwards it may yet find itself fallen into delusion or error. But this will be treated further on.

The divisions of method.—We will first touch upon *scientific method*, which may be used for teaching and in the composition of scientific books. It is twofold —*analytic* and *synthetic*.

(*a*) The *analytic method* proceeds from the whole to the parts of which the whole is composed, whence it is called *analytic* or *segregative*. And here it is important to observe that that conception which has most *comprehension* and least *extension* is, as it were, a whole which can be resolved into its parts, that is into conceptions of less *comprehension* and greater *extension*. For example, if I begin by treating of man, and then go on to the brutes, thence to plants, then to inorganic nature, and finally to universal corporeal substance, I shall be following the *analytic method*.

(*b*) The *synthetic method* proceeds from the parts to the whole, and thus from that which has least *comprehension* and greatest *extension* to that which has greatest *comprehension* and least *extension.* For example, if I begin with substance in the general, and so pass on, to minerals, to plants, to brutes, and finally to man, I shall be employing the *synthetic method,* so called because it *unifies* and *gathers together.*

It appears from the nature of these two methods that the *analytic* may be called *deductive,* and the *synthetic, inductive.*

The method that should be followed by the sciences. —Either we are treating of single sciences, or of philosophy as a whole. In the first case we said that the *synthetic method* is the most suitable, because in following it we are not obliged to assume as certain so many undemonstrated truths as we must if we pursue the *analytic method,* nor to repeat often the same things. In fact, it is the method that all the masters adopted. Hence geometry proceeds from the line to the circle, and not *vice versa.* Arithmetic from simple operations to the more complex. In physics we start from corporeal substance in general to end with man, and the same course is pursued in medicine, law, and all the other sciences. And when philosophy as a whole is treated, the *synthetic method* is to be followed, for the reasons already given, and this we intend to do. And since the *art of reasoning and philosophizing* is the fit preamble of philosophy, because before philosophizing we ought to know how to set about it, we will treat first of those notions which have less *comprehension* and greater *extension,* and therefore begin with *Primary Philosophy*; then of those which have greater *comprehension* and less *extension, i.e.,* corporeal substance in general and including man;

and, finally we will treat of God Who has the
greatest *comprehension* and no *extension*, because His
essence is single. We shall proceed thus in *speculative
philosophy*, and *practical* philosophy may be similarly
treated. This must be most specially insisted upon
in the present day, in order that knowledge may be
treated according to its nature as explained above.
Hence when we are dealing with *contingent* things,
where *essence* is distinct from *existence*, knowledge
should be occupied *primarily* with their *essence* and
only *secondarily* with their *existence*. The doctrine of
Plato and Aristotle that knowledge deals with necessary things is thus divinely interpreted by Aquinas:
" Knowledge treats of a thing in a twofold manner.
In one way *primarily* and *principally;* and in this
way it applies itself to the *universal causes* of things,
upon which it is founded. In the other it treats of a
thing *secondarily*, as it were in reflection, and it is
in this way that it applies itself to those things which
express these *universal causes*. . . . The learned
man makes use of the universal reason of things, as
a thing known and an instrument of knowledge. For
by means of *the universal reason of man*, I am able to
judge of this and of that. Now *universal reasons* of
things are all *immutable*, and therefore in this respect
knowledge is of *necessary things;* but when we speak
of the things which express these reasons, some are
necessary and *stable* (or *immutable* as God and that
which belongs to God) and some *contingent* and
unstable (or *mutable*), as it is in this way that knowledge can treat of things contingent and unstable "
(In Boet, De Trinit. Quæst v. art. 2): (2) When

science treats of God who is *single*, and in whom *essence* is not distinct from *existence*, it cannot treat primarily of the first, and as it were by *reflection* or application of the second., Hence *theology* must treat of God as *existent.*

What method applies to simple scientific cognitions. —Briefly we may say (1) when we wish to find out the truth of a proposition we may proceed by either method, the analytic or the synthetic, according as either may seem more convenient in each particular case. In the following demonstration I proceed by the *synthetic method. Every one who is injurious to his country is contemptible; but a rich miser is injurious to his country: therefore a rich miser is contemptible.* For I descend from notions of *less comprehension* and *greater extension* to notions of *greater comprehension* and *less extension.* Were I to take the opposite course, I should employ the *analytic method.* (2) We may also proceed from the *cause* to the *effect*, or from. the *reason* to *things reasoned of;* or from the *principle* to *that which it introduces*, and then our demonstration will be *à priori.* If we take the opposite course, it will be *à posteriori.* For example, *Man is endowed with reason: therefore he is free.* This is an *à priori* demonstration. But if I say *Man is free: therefore he is endowed with reason*, it will be *à posteriori*, because reason is the *principle* of *freedom.* (3) In simple demonstrations the rules given above are to be strictly observed, and thus every demonstration will be the expression (Lect. viii.) of the *principle* of *contradiction* which is the *criterion* of *truth.*

LECTURE XIV.—THE METHOD IN EXPERIENCE AND THE METHOD IN FAITH.

The method which should be pursued in particular experimental cognitions.—To form a *true* and *certain* judgment founded on experience, we must (1) distinguish the merely *cognitive faculty* from the *experimental faculty*. For example, an insane man, who cannot make this distinction, affirms that he has in his body or before his eyes that which really, is only in his imagination. (2) Consider what are the objects of each of the *experimental faculties.* The *spiritual affections* are objects of the *intellectual faculty*, which apprehends them, makes them present to itself (*direct consciousness*), and reflects upon them (*reflex consciousness*), judging with certainty of their existence. Those *internal sensible affections* are objects of the *internal sensitive faculty*, which modify it, *moving it sensibly*, which a *prolonged or continuous affection* does not do ; the *cause, place,* or *nature* of this *affection* is not an object of this faculty. For example, the pain that I feel in my body is an *object*, but that this pain is in my finger, or produced by a sharp instrument, or that it is the pain of inflammation, is not an object. Such judgments require discourse. Also in the external senses we must distinguish objects *proper* to each sense, objects *common* to several senses, or to all objects which are such *accidentally* (*per accidens* the ancients call them). For example, *colour* is the *proper object* of the *visual faculty, sound* of the *auditory*, &c. Distance and

size are common to several senses. Substance, cause,
and thousands of other things which *are connected*
with proper or common objects are called objects
per accidens. When any faculty in its congenial or
natural state is applied duly to its proper object it
cannot err; otherwise the error would recoil upon
the Author of nature, since if the faculties are rightly
disposed and applied to their proper objects, there is
no cause of error, and therefore no error. Therefore
a judgment founded on the report of a faculty expe-
riencing its *proper* object will be certainly true, nor
can it be denied without implicitly denying the
criterion of truth or the principle of contradiction.
With regard to *common* objects, there may doubtless
be a cause of error if the testimony of one sense only
is taken—as, for example, if any one were to judge
of distance by the eye alone. But if all the senses
are consulted which have relation to the object, there
will either be no cause of error (and therefore no
error), or if there be, the reason itself will be able to
discern it. If an oar immersed in water presents itself
to the eye as though it were bent, and therefore, as
to one of its parts, in a relation of *distance* which is
not the fact; since we are here dealing with a *common*
object, we are not content with the testimony of the
sight, but resort also to that of touch. The eye is
obliged to report as it does, otherwise it would not
duly present the object; but where objects are
common to several senses the reason must invoke
the testimony of all those concerned in order to have
certainty. Finally, in objects *per accidens* of the
senses error may indeed intrude itself, but this is not

to be attributed to experience. If, for example, I see in the distance a person dressed like a friend of mine, and I exclaim, " Here is my friend," but he turns out to be a stranger, have not the senses duly reported as they were bound ? Thus, in doctrines founded on experience there are often innumerable errors, because the senses are supposed to give their testimony where they really do not, that is, concerning things which are only their objects *per accidens.*

Nor can I here pass over in silence a rock upon which the votaries of the teachings of physical experience often split, which is the taking things for *causes* which are really not so, and in so doing appealing to experience or the testimony of the senses. But all that the senses can tell us of that which we call a cause (*their object per accidens*), is that it preceded or accompanied what we call the *effect.* The senses tell us *hoc post hoc,* or *hoc cum hoc,* but never *hoc ex hoc ;* and there is an indefinite difference between these formulas. But though it would take too long and would not suit our present purpose to discuss the point adequately, we think it will not be out of place to cite here one or two maxims of the celebrated Herschel, which agree with the Aristotelian doctrines (Hist. Animal l. 6. De animal. motione 1). Now, Herschel says that we have good reason to hold a thing to be the *cause* of a *fact* when (1) it invariably precedes the fact ; (2) when increased or diminished activity in the *cause* is followed by increase or diminution in the phenomenon which is judged to be its *effect ;* (3) when, my reason having examined the thing to see whether it can be produced by several *causes,* I find it can

have but one; if it can have several *causes* there is
no reason for ascribing the *effect* to one more than
another.

These are excellent rules, but we must also not
forget to inquire whether that which professes to be
the *cause* contains in any way the *effect;* for if this
be not the case it cannot absolutely be the *cause*, and
we must honestly confess that the *cause* is still hidden
from us, or we shall be in danger of falling into error.
Forgetful of this great principle some modern mate-
rialists have confounded the formula *hoc post hoc, hoc
cum hoc*, with the other formula, *hoc ex hoc*, as though
they were identical, and have reduced all the activities
of corporeal things to mere transpositions of con-
flicting movements; and made the organic arrangement of the parts the *reason* of the phenomena of life,
and the phosphorus in the brain the *cause* of thought.
Let us, then, use experience appropriately, and we
shall obtain *certainty* and *truth*, but never forget what
we said, that though *experimental cognition* is useful to
science, it can never itself be *truly called science.*

*The method to be employed in cognitions which rest
upon authority.*—Although the knowledge of truths
and facts which we obtain from authority is less
perfect than that which is gained by *science* and *experience*, still it is of very great value. The greater part
of mankind, either from want of intellectual power or
from their habits and occupations, are unable to
acquire the knowledge of many and most important
truths, whether in the speculative or practical order,
by any other way than that of faith; and in almost
all matters of fact we take the authority of others for

our guide, and believe. It is·by *faith* that we come to the knowledge of the ages that have preceded our own, and of places most distant from the sphere of our *experience*, which is confined to the narrow limits of the time and space in which we exist.

To make the act of faith prudent, and such as to eliminate all fear of 'error when the will determines the intellect to make it, it must be substantiated *by* *testimony* and by the *knowledge* and *veracity* of those who give it. This is the chief foundation, whether we are dealing with *speculative* or *practical truth* or with *facts*. For if the testimony that is given to us (whether *immediate*, or *mediate*, as in tradition) is accompanied by *knowledge* and *veracity* in those who give it, it cannot lead us into error. This is evident because error can only proceed from one of three causes, namely (1) if what we hear or read is not genuine testimony, but has been distorted, adulterated, mutilated, or falsified ; (2) if the person who gives it is deficient in information, and therefore did not know the truth or the fact ; (3) if he is wanting in veracity, and therefore lied.

With regard to *divine authority*, all that is required is that I know that what is ascribed to God has really been said by Him. When we have prudent reasons (*motives of credibility*) for being at rest upon this point, nothing more is needed, because there is intrinsic incompatibility between God and any deficiency in knowledge or veracity ; and therefore error is impossible. We say this whatever may be the objects of the divine testimony, whether *facts*, or *speculative* or *practical* truths, whether within or beyond the limits of nature. It is absurd, therefore, to endeavour to elude the irrefragable authority of the divine testimony with regard to certain natural facts or truths, by saying that God does not give revelation to teach us physics or philosophy. Whatever has the sanction of the word of God must be accepted by man with reverence as pure truth, because error is as repugnant to God as falsehood.

With regard to human authority, it is not sufficient to know the testimony and the person or persons who give it ; we must also be assured of the knowledge and veracity of the witnesses. Therefore, when we have to do with human *didactic* authority in truths which are difficult of comprehension, it is seldom that it yields us complete *certainty.* Nevertheless, we must remember the proverb : *Peritis in arte credendum.* But here we must consider the limitations to the knowledge of those who bear witness of the truth in question. For a clever mechanist will not, as such, be a good authority on medicine, nor need a man who is well versed in experimental physics or natural history be able to decide questions which belong to physical philosophy, nor are we bound to believe a very able chemist when he gives us a lecture on metaphysics.

In this matter we must keep in mind the following principles :

(*a*) A single authority, in a point of doctrine, is not in itself enough for certainty. I said *in itself* because we may have certainty in consideration of the arguments on which the authority rests, and the consent of many other learned men. It is plain that in this we do not include the authority of the Holy Father, because, according to Catholic doctrine, when he teaches dogma or morals as the universal Head of the Church, he is supported by the divine assistance which guides him to the truth. Therefore in such cases the authority of the Pope passes the bounds of human authority.

(*b*) The authority of many learned men in matters of pure doctrine may most justly produce certainty. I say pure to denote such as, for example, a mathematical proposition, a decision in morals, a principle of pure metaphysics. The concurrence of many learned men in the same judgment cannot be ascribed to chance, but must be caused by the light of the truth which shines upon their minds. Hence those are much to be blamed who despise the authority of the scholastic doctors, and prefer their own short-sighted judgments to those which have the unanimous consent of these.

Besides this, in relation to human authority concerning facts we must consider:

(*a*) That, generally speaking, we may hold it to be a prudent rule to accept it in practice. In fact, since we are almost constantly obliged to avail ourselves of the authority of others, it became the Divine Providence so to order things that we might not be perpetually led into error. Augustine said: "*Totam hominum vitam naturaliter in fide fundari*" (De Utilitate Credendi c. 12), and therefore he declared: "*Etsi auctoritate decipi miserum sit, longe tamen esse miserius ab eadem non commoveri*" (l. c. 16). In the second place we have experience

which has shown us that in following the authority
of others with regard to facts, we have very frequently found our canon to be right. In the third
place also where the facts in question are such as
are within the knowledge of any man who has
the ordinary use of his senses we cannot doubt
their testimony without also doubting their veracity.
But mendaciousness in man is exceptional; men do
not lie unless they expect to obtain some advantage
by it, and usually in each practical case it is not
difficult to discover whether there is any such
advantage to be obtained. So that in general we
may with prudence trust the authority of others.

(*b*) Often therefore human authority respecting
contemporaneous facts is such as to produce true
certainty. For in anything that rests on the authority
of others if it is clear that they possess knowledge,
or acquaintance with the facts and veracity, there
will be no cause of mistake or error present; and
therefore the effect cannot occur. That they have
knowledge will be plain because the witnesses have
the appropriate senses for perceiving the fact, and
because where they are numerous illusion is impossible. That there is veracity in the account of the
fact may often be known because a combination for
conspiracy among the witnesses would be impossible,
and they would derive no advantage from a lie.
Thus if the witnesses are sensible and upright men,
and there are several of them, and of contrary
opinions or tendencies, or conditions, even if one of
them might choose to lie, another certainly would not.

Therefore in many cases human authority can

produce certainty, because even if (in the abstract) the witnesses may be mistaken or false, still if they are either it will certainly be discovered.

(c) We may often have certainty on the authority of men about fact that occurred in past times. We shall have it when we are certain that there cannot have been any cause of error; since if the cause is taken away the effect cannot follow. Thus when a notable fact is in question and we are not treating of the minor accidents but of the substance of the fact and on all the lines of tradition we have concordant and respectable testimony (especially if it is confirmed by tablets and monuments) then we may without fear of error follow tradition. Thus the nature of the fact may be such as to warrant the argument: *the present generation admits it, therefore it happened;* or because the belief which exists in the present generation cannot be derived from a mere surmise of the generation which precedes it, but from a certain persuasion of the fact; and we may repeat this in every line of tradition (and the lines do not become extinguished or spring up suddenly but interlace each other) until we arrive at the period of the fact itself and have that testimony which is called ocular because the witnesses were present when it happened. Any one who wishes for a practical illustration of this line of argument will find one in the first of my three Conferences at Rome against the Protestants on the presence there of St. Peter.

If these principles were attended to, a host of scribblers and mendacious historians whose motives to untruthfulness are perfectly obvious would not obtain credit with their readers, and their writings would not have so many adherents. Above all, we ought not to suffer ourselves to be carried away by eloquent language or a sprightly style, and confound as so many do volubility and liveliness with truth. In the scientific pursuit of truth by means of experience, and still more of authority, the will must above all things be kept free from any passion which urges it to incline the intellect to embrace anything which it would not if left to itself. For although error being the privation of truth, resides where truth does, in the intellect, still it has its principal cause in the will. As a great doctor of philosophy sagaciously remarks (Suarez, Metaph. Disp. ix.), Speaking absolutely and with strict regard to the meaning of the terms, the intellect may be led by necessity to truth but never to falsehood. Therefore in all that concerns its exercise (or activity) it can never fall into a false judgment *except by virtue of the free impulse of the will*, since, excluding necessity, the intellect, not being free, cannot be determined to make a judgment except by the will. The reason of this distinction is that the intellect is not necessitated to form a judgment except by evidence of the thing known, as it exists in the fact or in the reason, because without evidence the object is not perfectly applied to the faculty, so as to act upon it necessarily and determine it ; now evidence cannot be the cause of a false judgment, because it is grounded in the thing itself, known as it is in itself, or else it is reducible to a few principles which are known and manifest in themselves. And from hence it follows that truth is far more immutable than falsehood; for a false judgment is mutable in its own nature, since the intellect whenever it pronounces a false judgment may change and pronounce the opposite and true one. But a true judgment, if it is perfect is immutable, even in creatures, because although there is nothing incompatible with change in it, for it may cease, yet in that to which 'it applies it cannot be changed by evidence into a false judgment. But it is of judgment on evidence that we speak; because if the judgment is arbitrary, however true it may be, the intellect, by virtue of the power of the will can turn and pronounce a false and opposite judgment. Now since in the will lies the principle cause of our errors, Dante's solemn warning (Par. xiii.) is most reasonable.

> And let this
> Henceforth be lead unto thy feet to make
> Thee slow in motion as a weary man,
> Both to the "yea" and to the "nay" thou seest not.
> For he among the fools is down full low,
> Whose affirmation, or denial, is
> Without distinction, in each case alike.
> Since it befalls, that in most instances
> Current opinion leads to false: and then
> Affection bends the judgment to her ply.
> Much more than vanity doth he loose from shore,
> Since he returns not such as he set forth
> Who fisheth for the truth and wanteth skill,
> And open proofs of this unto the world
> Have been afforded in Parmenides,
> Melissus, Bryso, and the crowd besides,
> Who journeyed on and knew not whither.

H

Thus we conclude our Logic, and in treating of it we have passed over many intricate questions usually discussed by modern teachers, holding that they only serve to make the study of philosophy wearisome to beginners. Such have need of milk, we repeat. The arduous questions of philosophy will be dealt with in their due time and place, that is when the pupil is able to understand them without serious difficulty, and when he can turn them to account.

Milton Keynes UK
Ingram Content Group UK Ltd.
UKHW032123140224
437808UK00004B/163